Yankee One
and George

Dave Brady

Cover design by Phil Green

**Police Review
Publishing Co. Ltd.**
14 St. Cross Street, London EC1N 8FE

ISBN 0 85164 013 3

Electronically typeset and printed by Heffers Printers Limited, Cambridge, England

CONTENTS

To Gigs, Michael and Alan.

Prologue

I LEARNED an early lesson in the basics of survival whilst serving in Korea with 41 Independent Commando Royal Marines, many years before joining the Metropolitan Police.

In November 1950 I was struggling through deep snow in bitter cold. I was swathed in layer after layer of heavy clothing, topped off with a thick fur-lined parka, the hood over my head. I was alone in mountains some miles north of an insigificant hamlet called Kotori. The night before had seen the emergence of thousands of Chinese from the hills. I was frightened. I stumbled through the snow, clumsy in my heavy winter footwear. The conditions seemed to nullify my years of training, I was very tired and was an easy target for any wandering Chinese soldier who may have felt inclined to kill me.

After having been assured some short hours before that the war was over, and that we had won, my morale was a little low! 'Home for Christmas,' we had been told by no less a personality than General MacArthur. He was the governor, he should know. I was somewhat nonplussed by recent events. Was it only eight hours ago that my mess tin had been brimming with turkey and all the trimmings, air-dropped by a fat bellied supply plane? To celebrate American Thanksgiving, we were told. Thanksgiving? What, for Christ's sake, had we to be thankful for ? 'Here I am,' I thought to myself, 'all alone, my unit decimated, lots of my mates dead, Chinese everywhere. Someone had made a momentous cock up.'

I patted my pockets. Somewhere were my morphine syringes. I wondered whether the needle would penetrate my layers of clothing, let alone my skin. Still, if the worst came to the worst the morphine would alleviate the pain, if I were wounded, whilst I slowly froze to death.

The night, well illuminated by the moon and flares, had been a bloody nightmare. Men were dying, but not in the patriotic Hollywood way, with softly spoken, brave speeches. Men were screaming and calling for their mothers with accents from as far apart as London and New York. I saw, in the half light, to my distress, men throwing their weapons to the snow, arms raised high. I didn't blame them, I realised that the game was up. I couldn't see any green berets at all and hoped that I was not the only one left.

We had set out with high hopes as 'Force Drysdale,' named after our colonel, mixed Yank and British marines. We were to fight our way through to some trapped Yank marines at a place called Hagaru, to bring them out. The task was eventually accomplished, but my part of the force was split from the rest, surrounded, and virtually wiped out. I decided not to surrender, but to try to get back to Kotori, our starting point to the south. 'Which way is south? Sod it, I don't know.' I stumbled away, talking to myself, crouched and scared. I couldn't rush, I did not dare sweat. To sweat with excessive exertion beneath the heavy clothing could perhaps kill you later on as the sweat froze.

The sound of battle diminished, I was leaving it behind. No heartstopping whine as bullets splashed nearby. The sounds stopped completely as the last few surrendered.

'Christ, what's that?' From a ditch immediately in front of me a figure appeared. He was close. As his arm arched I saw the object he had thrown, loop towards me. His frightened expression belied all the tales I had heard of the inscrutable oriental. His quilted jacket and starred cap revealed him to be a Chinese soldier. The object he had thrown plopped into the snow some eight feet beyond me. It was a grenade . . . I was engulfed in fear, none of my past life flashed before me, just stark fear. I threw myself to the ground. Silence. No bang, no death. I cautiously peeped up. The bloody thing had not gone off!

'Where's the chink?'

I heard the crunch of snow and I lay still, waiting. In an instant he was up on his feet and stumbling away. I saw he had no weapon. His bottle had obviously gone and he perhaps thought I was stalking him after the misfire of his grenade. Without hesitation I shot him, dead, with no qualms and definitely no regrets.

My escape and survival is another story, but it may seem

strange that this episode, whilst serving in the Marines, should have helped me in my police service. I remembered and used the Chinese soldier as a reminder always.

The chink who threw the grenade dropped me deeply in the shit. I survived through considerable good fortune, but I ensured that he wouldn't have the opportunity to do it again. This philosophy is equally as important for survival in the police environment as it is in war. For police work is war, much subtler than military warfare, but almost as dangerous.

Chapter 1   The Day War Broke Out

'HE looks like Rudolph Hess used to look,' I thought to myself. I peered from around the rear end of a police car. I was on one knee, filled with curiosity and just a little windy. The object of my attention was crouched in the rear seat of a Ford Corsair which had, fairly recently, been rammed by a police car. Both cars had come to a violent stop at the entrance to a cul-de-sac. Rudolph, the focus of my attention, was one of two men in the car. The other man was in the driver's seat. Each of them was holding a sawn-off shotgun.

Five minutes earlier I had been quietly patrolling in my police car, in Hornsey, a rather squalid part of north London, but a superb place to learn the trade of policing. I was alone, as I liked to be, and fairly content with my lot. I was performing the function I loved, that of a street copper, out on my own. I had about 20 years of experience behind me, and no desire for promotion.

The drone of radio transmissions eased into my ears and were dismissed as irrelevant to my patrol area, until: 'The bastards are shooting at us!' Ryan's voice, distorted by static, urgent and excited, blared from my radio.

'Where are you Ryan?'

'Mountview Road, towards Crouch Hill . . . four up . . . Ford Corsair . . . it's all over the road . . . two at least armed with shotguns.' The staccato conversation ceased, and my imagination took off.

I felt a twinge of alarm, changed down a gear and accelerated as fast as I could towards my mate Ryan and his crew. Static rustled again from the radio, the transmission button was being pressed. Then a boom which could only be put down to the discharge of a shotgun. More static, then Ryan, somewhat breathless, shouted into his microphone, 'Sparsholt Road, urgent assistance.'

In police parlance there are various set phrases to indicate, as succinctly as possible, the current situation. For instance, if, on the personal radio, the officer first on the scene announced, 'LOB' over the air, this indicated to other officers who might be on their way at a fair rate of knots, that the situation was far from serious. In fact, it told all and sundry that the call was 'A load of balls.'

The most important call was 'Urgent Assistance.' This indicated that the copper was deeply in the tripe. It was never broadcast lightly, as the sender was aware that police would break their necks to get there a quickly as possible. To hear a call from Ryan David for assistance was a rarity. He was a large, aggressive, competent Welshman, If he needed help then he was in deep bother.

I was, by now, racing through the traffic. I was suffering from a mixture of emotions, mostly anxiety for my mates, who were obviously in some trouble, coupled with the old adrenalin flow, which was one of the reasons why police work held such fascination for me. If, as a driver, you have not had the pleasure of driving very fast through crowded streets, with the traffic ahead of you opening up like the Red Sea for Moses, then you've never lived. It is all part of the second childhood syndrome, the cops and robbers fantasy.

I drove over the crest of Crouch Hill, the wheels momentarily losing contact with the road surface, and then, down the hill, like a bat out of hell towards Ryan and his crew.

In the distance I could see the flash, flash of blue lights from a posse of police cars, unoccupied and at various angles on the road. I stopped my car about 30 yards short of all the activity and ran towards, I didn't know what! I was soon to find out!

As I trotted to the corner I could see coppers crouched behind various motor cars. The nearest to me was Steve Hughes. He was slightly pale around the gills. He had every right to be as he had only arrived at Hornsey nick the same morning, straight from Hendon Training School. His head popped up from behind a panda car. He waved his hand, palm downwards, in a 'Get down' motion. Then he pointed and I needed no second telling to keep my head down.

There was a Ford Corsair, shabby and battered, containing the two men, one in the front seat and 'Rudolph Hess' in the back. Both waving shotguns.

Walking slowly away from the car, unarmed, as were we all,

was Station Sergeant Mick Peffer. Prior to my arrival he had walked up to the car, from which shots were being fired at police, and attempted to talk them into surrender. They had refused and threatened to shoot him. I was extremely grateful that they hadn't taken Mick as a hostage, it would have made things much more difficult, but I admired his bottle at the time.

The first call had referred to 'four up.'

'Where are the other two?' I called out.

Steve pointed again, this time to where Ryan, with a triumphant grin on his face, was sitting on a man on the pavement. The man seemed to be unconscious. There was nothing too unusual about that, folk who tangled with Ryan seemed to end up in that condition more often than not!

The boom of the shotgun made me start. I saw that Ryan was holding his arm awkwardly but still sitting astride the unconscious villain.

'Are you OK Ryan?' I called.

'Better off than this bastard!' he yelled in reply, pressing down on his prisoner. I looked towards the Corsair, the bang had been Rudolph firing his gun.

I heard the whine of a starter motor and with some anxiety, I realised that the noise came from the villains' car. There was a crash of reluctant gears and the Corsair jerked backwards as Rudolph's mate, who was in the driver's seat, attempted to free it from the close embrace of Ryan's unoccupied police car. What could I do? The last thing I wanted to happen was for the bastards to drive off in a shower of shotgun fire and escape.

I would definitely recognise Rudolph again, having had a prolonged look at him. Identification parades were always dicey though, because, no matter how certain one was, allegations always flew about like confetti, so it was always best to capture the villains, if possible, in situ.

I suddenly realised that I was up and running towards Ryan's abandoned Rover police car. There was a blast of sound as a shotgun was fired. With a shock it occurred to me that the bastard was shooting at me, dear old Rudolph again.

Coupled with the boom I felt a gentle stinging on my forehead and I stopped momentarily. The weight of my fat body propelled me on again towards the police car.

'You stupid old bastard,' I said to myself. Fear tinged with anger swept over me. Rudolph was definitely not messing about.

The Corsair was, by now, on the move, in reverse and heading for the open road beyond the cul-de-sac. I stopped, and like a pratt of a copper in an old 'B' movie I drew my truncheon and threw it wildly in the general direction of the villains' car. It clanged uselessly against the car door.

'Bollocks!' I thought. What a stupid useless thing to do. The villains were now heading towards a gap in the police cars and to freedom. They were blasting off the occasional cartridge from their sawn-offs to discourage any interference. Rudolph was loving it, he was looking around all the time and letting off the odd shot or two. The expression on his face was one of absolute triumph, he just knew he was going to make it. This, for some reason made me extremely angry.

Breathing heavily from a mixture of fear, adrenalin and 50 years of nicotine addiction, I found myself, to my surprise sitting in Ryan's Rover, with the arse of the police car pointing at the Corsair and some 20 yards from it. Rudolph was grinning and waving his shotgun about in apparent glee at their impending escape. His mate was performing a sort of three point turn. Something was trickling into my right eye, I touched it and looked at my finger. Blood. The bastard! I had to have him now!

My fumbling fingers couldn't find the ignition key, or even the switch, panic!

'Ryan, where's the fucking key?' I screamed.

'In the ignition, you daft bugger,' his Welsh accent heightened and excited. He had a rough idea of my intentions, but couldn't have assisted me had he wanted too, for his prisoner was beginning to regain consciousness.

Where, where is the bloody ignition switch? Ah, there it was, thank God. I twisted the key savagely. The three and a half litre engine roared into life. All that I could see in my mind's eye was the triumphant leer on the face of Rudolph. By now I was performing without thinking. It was as though I was looking on at another idiot. The automatic gear grated into reverse, with maximum revs from the engines as I pressed my foot fiercely down on the accelerator, my other foot hard on the footbrake. The noise was unbelievable, I wasn't doing the car any favours, but I was building up maximum power before I took off. I looked forward to the pleasure of presenting Rudolph with a ton of motor car at a fairly fast speed.

I twisted around in the seat, holding the driver's door open in case I had to bale out in a hurry with half a ton of buckshot up my arse! Whoops! The Rover was now hurtling backwards, very very fast, much too fast for any further effective control over the damn thing.

With my foot flat on the floor I could see the Corsair looming large in my vision. It was broadsides to me, the driver desperately swinging the steering wheel. There was Rudolph again, he was looking straight at me with a very cross expression on his face. I thought again what an evil looking bastard he was. As the short distance between us closed very rapidly, he screwed his eyes up as he brought up the sawn-off shotgun and peered along the short barrel. The bore of the gun looked like the Mersey Tunnel.

It is difficult to recall emotions at such times. On this occasion it was really true that the world seemed, if not to stand still, at least the actions slowed down somewhat. I remember thinking that it might all end here. How many coppers had found themselves in similar situations before me? I started to shout, what the subject matter was I will never know. I now know why the Japanese army always scream 'Banzai' during an attack. The mere exertion of yelling helps to diminish fear.

I braced myself for the impending collision as I was now about 10 feet from the bandit car and closing fast! A gigantic red flash filled my vision and the back of the car seemed to distintegrate with the combined efforts of a close-range shot and the rending of metal as the Rover buried itself into the side of the Corsair. Beyond it I could see a large police van, which was ramming the car from the other side. He was travelling forward and not in reverse as I was. Examining Ryan's car which I had used as a battering ram, after the fracas was over, I discovered that the shotgun had blown a hole in the lid of the boot about six inches lower than the bottom sill of the rear windscreen and about six inches below the back of my head!

As the shot was fired I felt a stinging sensation in my right hand. Rudolph had struck again. I didn't like him very much. Try as I may I cannot remember the next few seconds. The first moment of recollection was to find myself standing beside the rear nearside passenger door of the Corsair. There were coppers everywhere in full cry. I heard a sharp crack; that was no shotgun, it sounded like a pistol,

'Christ, if they've got one of those I'm going home!'

I pulled at the car door, the bloody thing would not budge. There was a brief moment of some anxiety and just a tinge of panic as I saw Rudolph, still holding his shotgun, staring at me from the other side of the glass. He was not looking quite so defiant now, but nevertheless still a mite dangerous to say the least. I desperately wrenched at the door, and, to my relief, it opened at last, 'Ah, there you are you bastard!' I shouted at Rudolph. He was laying, face uppermost, on the rear seat of the car. He was surrounded by debris and broken glass. The stubby, evil looking shotgun cradled across his chest. I was aware of other coppers dragging the villain from the front seat, but Rudolph was mine!!

There was an excited babble of confused noise, some of the language extremely explicit.

'It's all up,' he gasped.

'Too right it is,' I shouted. I was very angry and yet exhilarated at the possibility of nicking Rudolph. I leaned over him, watching the gun with the fascination of a politician bending over a voter's baby. Rudolph's face became blood-stained and I realised that most of it was mine. I was casually dripping all over him.

I had a truncheon in my hand, where did that come from? With every ounce of energy I could summon I flayed Rudolph across the face with the truncheon. I did not, thank you, want him to do any further naughties with the gun. I felt that the imposition of pain, as soon as possible and as hard as possible, would, perhaps discourage him from further attempts to do me a mischief.

There was frenzied activity in the rear passenger compartment. Everything seemed to be happening at tremendous speed. All that could be heard was the sound of our heavy breathing and the scratching noise of our combined weight on the upholstery. Similar sounds must often have been heard in a Cairo brothel. One more swipe with the truncheon and Rudolph began to lose interest. His face split like a peach and he released his hold on the gun which rolled onto the floor in front of the seat. However it was still a little too close to Rudolph's hands as he continued to struggle. I had realised by now that he could not be trusted really to behave like an English gentleman, so, for good measure and with a great deal of satisfaction, I hit him again. By now our rates of bleeding were about equal and as honours were even, I desisted.

A phalanx of blue clad dervishes descended upon him. Coppers in full cry are a fearsome sight, these coppers, all mates of mine, were very angry. They had been on the receiving end of a positive fusilage of shots and, unlike politicians, could not make lucid speeches about such situations. Coppers had to deal with them, on the street and for real, not with pompous hindsight! The real reason for their anger was that Ryan and I had been damaged by the irresponsible and random fire that Rudolph had initiated.

I sat down on the pavement, all bravado gone and the realisation of what might have been causing a paling of my complexion. I felt considerable satisfaction within myself, coupled with a wee bit of egotism rearing its ugly head. I was soon snatched back to reality, when, red faced and apparently frustrated I saw, trudging towards me, Terry Southwell, a copper from Hornsey nick. He was carrying a police service revolver.

'Dave,' he said quietly, 'You really were a bloody nuisance, every time I tried to shoot one of those buggers before they shot one of you, your fat arse got in the way. The one shot I did get off wasn't too far from you.'

It was then I remembered the sharp crack that I had heard. Christ, if I'd known it was a copper, even Terry, who was pointing a shooter in my direction, I would have run a mile!

I stood up rather shakily, feeling my 47 years bearing down on me, as Ryan David, the Welsh instigator of the affair came running up to me. At last I discovered that Rudolph and his three mates had carried out an armed robbery at a Post Office shortly before Ryan and other coppers had poked their noses in. Ryan shouted, but then, in the many episodes in which we had been involved together, Ryan *always* shouted.

'The big one in the sky, boyo,' he roared.

He gestured in the air with his fist like an Arsenal forward who has just scored against Spurs. His other arm hung limply by his side. He had also been injured, but our aches and pains disappeared in the exuberance of the moment. We shook hands, a ridiculous and melodramatic thing to do but it seemed right at the time.

The journey back to the nick took place in a self-congratulatory daze. Lucidity returned when I was standing in the CID office at Hornsey nick. The police station was crawling with all sorts of coppers and bossmen, they had gathered as the news of the event filtered through various offices. Ann Patrick, a woman detective, approached me with a large tumbler of scotch. I wolfed it back, it tasted bloody marvellous! Then I had another and another. The initial feeling of elation began to evaporate and I was beginning to feel a little fragile! The police surgeon bustled into the office carrying the customary little black bag. I had stopped bleeding as the time had progressed and in a semi-drunken stupor I gazed at the surgeon as he probed about in my head and hand.

'Why isn't he hurting me?' I thought.

Chapter 2   Off on the Wrong Foot

THE place, Beak Street, in the West End of London. In 1955 this was the reception and recruiting centre for the Metropolitan Police. A brown, ugly building, even on a bright day in September. The Royal Marines, my haven for the past 12 years was now behind me. I recognised that the aggressive, shouting police sergeants were of exactly the same ilk as their counterparts in the Marines. The disinfectant smells which permeated through the rooms had a familiar ring about them. I had a brief touch of the seconds . . . shall I go through with this? I thought of my wife, Gigs, cooped up in a tiny room in Peckham with my young son Michael. I wished that I was with them.

A huge, red faced sergeant stalked into the room exuding self confidence to a nauseating degree. The dozen or so of us waiting and sharing mutual apprehension, looked at him uneasily.

'In there,' he roared, 'are doctors. They want to know if you lot are warm and breathing.' He grinned sardonically, enjoying his feeble joke. We all laughed dutifully.

'You will strip off in here, wrap yourselves in one of those towels over there and come in again when your names are called. OK?'

We all nodded. Not a word was spoken.

'At one stage the doctor will ask you to turn around and bend over. For some reason that escapes me, he will want to look up your arse. Don't be coy, just do as you are told.'

'Brady!' My turn. I had seen that most of the budding coppers waiting with me were large muscular men, I felt some trepidation as, in those days I was tall, but very thin. I walked into the room. A bare trestle table was the sole item of furniture and seated behind it were two men, dressed in white coats. Their dress indicated to the layman that here were no ordinary mortals, but beings with the magical qualities of being able to right the agonies of piles, venereal disease and other sundry ailments that tend to predominate in an all male society.

The older of the two gazed at me through watery, weak eyes. His boredom apparent. The usual flow of questions designed to probe my medical history with the minimum of effort on his part, issued from his lips.

Then, suddenly, he said,

'Turn . . .' before he could complete the question I decided to impress him with the speed of my reactions. I let the towel around my middle drop to the floor. Spinning round I bent over and presented my far from attractive bum for his inspection . . . 'the palms of your hands towards me,' as he completed his request his voice became strident with surprise. I straightened myself, red faced, and turned to face him.

'I see from your papers that you were in the Marines, is that so?'

'Yes Sir,' I replied.

'Well Brady, to show your arse at the slightest provocation, may have been suitable behaviour in the Marines, but, in the police force, if you are accepted, you will lose both the respect of your brother officers, and your virginity, if you cannot learn to conquer this unfortunate tendency.'

The other doctor spoke not a word.

Long minutes later I left the examining room and heard a roar of laughter from the doctors as I closed the door. I was mortified. A large ex-matelot from Yorkshire, who was next, said: 'What was all that about, lad?'

I decided that the only comment I could offer which would demonstrate my command of the English language as I looked him straight in the eye was, 'Bollocks!'

After a written examination, which I felt would not tax a 10-year-old, and an interview conducted by four senior officers, I was pronounced suitable material to be moulded and slapped into shape, hopefully to emerge as a constable of the Metropolitan Police.

*   *   *

As the police coach approached Hendon Training School, I could see, in the distance, a collection of huts, a far cry from the modern Hendon high-rise buildings which mass produce coppers of whom at least 25 per cent are women. In the mid-'50s there was hardly a building over two stories high, and hardly a woman in sight.

There was a military atmosphere about the place. I did not realise that all training establishments in the police had this aura. Having had 12 years of discipline in the Marines, I was not too sure whether I had done the right thing in joining. I was older than the average intake, and the blokes I was going to train with seemed callow. Still I had to earn a crust to survive in civvy street, and this was as good a way as any to earn it.

The living accommodation was in clean and prison-like barrack rooms. I slept fitfully that first night and wondered what the morning would bring. No reveille bugle sounded, but there was a similarity, a loud sergeant roared into the room at about 6.30 in the morning and shouted us into consciousness. The breakfast was as horrible as I expected it to be. I didn't eat the first one, but hunger made me force down subsequent meals. At a quarter to nine it was time to move off to the barracks square, where the morning parade was to take place.

There I was, at last, on the parade ground at Hendon Police Training School, with a smattering of seasoned men amongst hundreds of fresh faced lads. The blue uniforms fresh and creased, rookies all. The more seasoned recruits, with at least three weeks in the job, were looking down disdainfully on the latest intake, of which I was a part. The helmets were worn, not with the confidence of the coppers we see patrolling our streets, but rather, perched uncomfortably, like blue pisspots, wobbling uncertainly with every movement of the head. Ungainly and slightly comical.

I stood there, scratching myself with not a sergeant in sight. My squad mates, of various shapes and sizes but mostly rather large in stature, shuffled uncomfortably. A sombre and slightly nervous silence pervaded the parade ground. I noticed, in the far corner two wooden tripods with a length of timber, not unlike a telegraph pole, stretched between the tripods. In search of a way to break the nervous silence, I wandered across and perused the assorted timbers. The horizontal pole was painted red and white as though it should have been a protrusion outside a barber's shop. It reminded me of a caber.

I pinched my nose with my forefinger and thumb and made a loud wailing noise through my nose. By striking, at the same time, my Adam's apple repeatedly with the right of my hand, whilst continuing to wail, I produced what I fondly imagined to be a fair imitation of the skirl of a bagpipe. Immediately my new found comrades copied my antics and to my pleasure, a cacophony of hideous noise blasted across the parade ground. I lifted the red and white pole and grappled it into position, cupping the end in my palms with the point skywards.

Screaming like a dervish, I galloped across the square, finally heaving the pole into the air with all my might. As it soared into the blue the raucous rendering of *Highland Laddie* changed to a cheer from the throaty pipe band. Slowly and majestically the pole turned in the air. As it struck the ground it shattered into pieces. The wails faded away to be replaced by the sound of stampeding feet. I looked around, all the budding coppers were doing what is known in police parlance as 'a runner'!

I had, therefore, established at a very early stage in my career, that whilst things were going well you would be surrounded by eager supporters, but, when things looked decidedly dicey, the erstwhile close friends would evaporate into the wind, not to reappear until the dust had settled!

Groups of grinning recruits were scattered around the edge of the parade ground. I quickly gathered together the shattered remains of the pole.

'Hurry up Brady,' I said to myself, 'Before some officious bastard appears.'

I carefully placed the pieces together on the ground as though assembling a jigsaw puzzle. My hope was that when I have finally completed positioning the bits together, the first bastard to pick it up would get the blame, when it fell asunder. There I was on my hands and knees, busy. As I positioned the last shattered remains I saw, to my horror, three feet away from my nose, not one, but two extremely shiny pairs of boots. As my gaze travelled upwards I passed along blue razor sharp creases. Up and up, past two rather rotund bellies and then, dismay, sergeant's stripes positively shimmering with pleasurable anticipation. Finally two very red and angry faces.

'You pratt, that pole was a dummy horse!' the larger of the two screamed.

'We use it to teach fucking idiots like you how to deal with an injured horse.'

I stood up and brushed my knees,

'A horse?'

'Yes, a horse. The bloody thing has been there since about nineteen hundred, you've been here one day and you've broken the bastard. What's your name?'

I told him as my mind raced. No way out of this, fancy getting the sack after just one day. What will I tell Gigs? The man's right, I am a pratt.

Then there I was, in the holy of holies, the Chief Superintendent's office. Lots of coppers never saw the inside of this place throughout their careers and yet, here I was on my first day.

'Well, what have you to say?' He was all gold braid and moustache.

'I didn't think it was quite so fragile, Sir.' God sneered at me,

'You will pay two pounds eight shillings for the pole and I will be watching you!'

I shuffled out of his office. Joy . . . no sack! Christ, two pounds eight shillings out of a weekly pay of seven pounds. I swore to myself that this would be the last time that I would piss about and show off. A forlorn hope of course, I always pissed about throughout my service. Boss men continued to keep an eye on me, somewhat benevolently, in view of the fact that the skylarking was always coupled with bloody hard work on my part. The debunking of authority is always much more satisfactory in a disciplined organisation.

The training I underwent at Hendon in the mid-'50s was

very basic. Nothing about the variations of behaviour expected in dealing with ethnic minorities. In fact, I'm not even sure
that the phrase 'ethnic minorities' had been invented. We
were just taught right and wrong. No one bothered us with the
reasons that caused people to commit crime. We concentrated
on what we could do to stop people committing crime, and
what we could do if, despite all our efforts, they went ahead
and committed it. The only racial element in the training
appeared to be the constant personification of the Jewish taxi
driver as the man most likely to upset police. Jewish taxi
drivers, according to our instructors, stopped on pedestrian
crossings, short changed customers, ignored red lights, and
probably plotted against the Queen and Government. I was a
bit surprised at all this, especially as we'd just been in a war
against a man with similar opinions about Jews.

The instructors' special delights were what they called the
'Breathing Acts'. They were the Metropolitan Police Act and
the Vagrancy Act. According to the instructors, some of
whom might have prospered in the Gestapo, 'They mean that
if you're breathing, you can be nicked.' But the people they
wanted nicking more than anyone else seemed to be the
motorist. That caused me a lot of problems at the time. I
thought our first targets would be thieves, rapists, burglars,
but no, most of the training was directed at how to summons
motorists. Quite sensible, when you come to think of it,
because motorists kill more people than thieves or burglars.

With all this propaganda about Jewish taxi drivers, I left
training school with the will to deal with this menace to our
society. In the succeeding 25 years, I never found one. I came
across a lot of Jewish taxi drivers, but they were always the
injured party; they got cheated, they got robbed, and I can
honestly say I've never come across a passenger who claimed
that he'd been cheated by a cabbie. This somewhat destroyed
my belief in the infallibility of instructors, who were quite
happy in the training school, but not so bloody hot at practical
policing. I make no apology for saying that most of the
instructors I knew in the Metropolitan Police were the type of
copper that I would rather not be involved with at street level.

The end of the training school period was all a bit blurred, as Gigs, my wife, was in hospital, and I had to get someone to look after our young son, as well as organise the move from our room in Peckham to police married quarters in Hornsey. But with that accomplished, I set out for what was to be my workplace, office, factory, my harbour for the next 25 years, Hornsey Police Station.

*   *   *

It was scruffy, Victorian and every brick reeked of atmo-sphere. I loved it! What impressed me most of all was sitting in the station yard: a large, black powerful car, it was, I was soon to learn, 'The Area Car,' the workhorse of the nick, the response vehicle for emergency calls and, in those years driving an area car was considered by the working coppers to be a cream job. I gazed at this vehicle and looked out of the corner of my eye at the crew, two large, competent, hard, experienced police officers. I longed for the years to fly past so that I too could inspire a little confidence rather than be a mere rookie.

I wanted area car duty so very badly that it became a greater ambition than promotion or further advancement. I thought of how satisfying it would be to rescue the public from their trials and tribulations at the hands of the criminal classes. My naïve daydreams faded away when I suddenly remembered, I couldn't drive!

Time made me realise that the real work horses of any police station were the ordinary beat coppers. None of the glamour of leaping about in high powered motor cars, none of the supercharged *Sweeney* influence, just steady hard work on their patch. The local Bobby, with his accumulated knowledge of his own people can pick his way carefully through the human debris, dusting some down and standing them up again, heaving some to one side as beyond redemption and occasionally nicking the more criminally infectious, to remove their corrupting influence, either to the prison, or better still, on to some other bugger's patch!

I went the way of all police flesh, starting out by summonsing motorists for offences for which in later police life, I would issue a mild bollocking. Then, at long last, my first arrest. With considerable misery I was patrolling, on foot in the early hours of a November morning. I was quite pissed off and my desire to clean up London had become sadly diminished!

I heard running footsteps, which quickened as they approached me from behind,

'Officer . . . Thank God!' the lady, in her late thirties and apparently more angry than upset, pointed back in the direction from which she had approached,

'A dirty bastard back there has just indecently exposed himself to me!' She turned and started to hurry back, I followed, heavily swathed in a large overcoat and covered with a wobbling helmet. I followed her, eager to say something which would impress her and to reassure her that by God, she was safe now. I was so knackered trying to keep up with her I couldn't utter a word. . . .

A figure loomed out of the darkness, her devil may care attitude evaporated, she lept backwards, and squeaked, 'That's him.'

I nervously cleared my throat as I approached the man. He was extremely small and my bravery increased with my awareness of his stature. I peered at him through the semi-dark, prepared my face into what I fondly presumed was its most effective inquisitional expression, and swaggered slightly as I prepared the question which was going to cause his defences to crumble and deliver himself, pleading guilty, into my custodial arms.

He smacked me straight on the nose. Christ it hurt, my eyes watered and I reached towards him, he was really in the shit now! He had hit a copper! I grabbed air, he was away on his toes. He raced off down the alley-way with the full majesty of the law in hot pursuit. As I ran I started to try and shrug off my overcoat. It was impossible. I was neither gaining on him, nor losing him. It was a situation which indicated that in the near future we would both collapse exhausted. Then I saw a large

lad, leaning against a garden wall on a corner, past which my
running flasher would just have to gallop. 'Stop that man . . .'
I shouted, if I could have found it I would probably have blown
my whistle to give the request added authority.

The effect was astounding. The lounging lad immediately
stepped forward, adopting a John L. Sullivan pose, with legs
wide apart and both fists held at face level above bended
elbows. The flasher slowed momentarily and with a mighty
haymaker knocked the lad to the ground, before jumping over
him with the alacrity of an Aintree racehorse. I went arse over
tit over the recumbent man and we both did ourselves serious
mischiefs trying to leap to our feet. The flasher disappeared,
never to be seen again. The lad disappeared. I struggled to my
feet and made my breathless way back to the poor lady who
had been the subject of the flash. She also had disappeared. I
was completely alone. I was a little upset, it shouldn't have
happened this way. I wandered disconsolately back to the
police box at the far end of my beat. There I met an old copper
to whom I related the sad tale. Upon his advice, after he had
made a few phone calls from the box I forgot the whole affair.
It was good advice, I never heard any more. I soldiered on
with varying degrees of success until at last, after numerous
courses I paraded for duty as the driver of the area car . . . my
police life had at last really begun.

Chapter 3   Dramatic Liberty

MY first assignment on the area car was to an establishment to which the police were seldom called, 'The Mountview Theatre Club.' As the name implied it was arty in character and, as such, its habitues tended to solve their own problems rather than have anything whatsoever to do with the local constabulary.

You can therefore imagine my surprise one winter's afternoon, when the radio crackled out a message indicating that police were urgently required at the club, where a man had been stabbed! I should explain that the club was not a drinking establishment but in fact a theatre where students were trained in the noble art of acting.

I raced to the scene and as I arrived a very anxious man was waiting at the main door of the theatre. His fluttering hands and his inability to stand still indicated that not only was there an emergency, but also that he was not over endowed with masculine attributes.

'This way officer, hurry please,' he glanced over his shoulder as he trotted through into the building.

There was no sign, at this stage, of an ambulance. I desperately ran through my mind the various treatments for stab wounds so I hurried back to my car for the first aid box containing, I hoped, a large pad dressing. I then retraced my steps and hurried after the informant. We rushed along shabby corridors and through a battered door. I have never really understood the fascination for the greasepaint atmosphere of the stage or the hunger for audience approval, but, once having passed through the door, the transformation from shabby surroundings to medieval splendour was almost a physical shock.

There, in front of me, brilliantly lit, was what was apparently a castle banqueting hall, the figures milling about on the stage were gaudily attired in period costume. One man was standing with an anguished expression on his face. In his right hand he carried a sword and in his left a long dagger. The tip of the gleaming dagger glistened crimson with what was either blood or a very good dramatic substitute.

In front of him lying face down was another man, crying hysterically, 'Look what the silly bugger's done, just look!' he lisped rather badly. I thought this must have been an impediment to his theatrical abilities.

I looked, and saw that his nicely rounded bum, encased in theatrical tights, was bleeding copiously slightly to the right of centre.

'It was an accident, I am really ever so sorry,' minced the man with the dagger.

I felt that, prior to first aid, it would probably be a good idea to relieve the dagger man of his weapon. So I reached out and took it from him. He gazed at me with large round eyes brimming with tears. We were both, at that time, speechless.

I leaned over the bleeding figure whilst at the same time removing a dressing from the first aid box. I gently placed the dressing over the wound. He winced.

'Tell me officer, how bad is it?'

His anxiety was obvious, his injury, if in the wrong place could obviously greatly affect both his future social and love life.

'It'll be OK,' I whispered, 'He's caught you right of centre.'

'Thank Christ for that!' His tears suddenly changed and he began to giggle with relief.

'You had better stay as you are until the ambulance arrives,' I told him.

I turned to his alleged assailant and asked how the incident had occurred.

'Well, we were doing a duelling scene,' he said. 'I was supposed to pass the sword under his armpit so that it would look as though he had been stabbed. As I lunged forward with the sword, he lifted his arm. He stumbled and half turned, I was so anxious about the sword that I moved it out of the way and pushed him off with my other hand, I forgot I had a dagger in it and I stabbed him up the arse!'

He smiled as he completed his sad tale, it was all too much for me, I burst out laughing, the tears streamed down my cheeks, I clutched my stomach. Finally I managed to control my amusement only to turn away and see the gorgeously dressed victim still lying patiently on the floor with a huge wound dressing pointing to the sky from his rotund rear.

I pressed my lips tightly together and with a huge effort of will managed to control myself until a plaintive voice manifested itself from the other end of the wound dressing,

'I'm glad you think it's funny, Officer!'
As he spoke he rolled over onto his back pressing the wound firmly against the floor. He let out a squeal of pain and began to sob. At that moment the ambulance crew arrived.

'What you got mate?' from the ambulance man.

'This geezer here,' I told them pointing to the victim, 'has been stabbed in the arse by that geezer there,' pointing to the assailant.

'What with?' smirked the ambulance man.

Again roars of laughter echoed through the area, this time the ambulance man and the assailant joined in.

The victim, forgetting his injury leapt to his feet in a paroxym of rage, 'You bastards, you bastards, it's not fucking funny, you can all piss off!' He slumped into a chair, having gone pale from his exertions. As he did so he again forgot the location of his wound and with a scream leapt from the chair clutching his rectum to subside, face down, in his original prone position.

The ambulance crew withdrew for a moment and returned with a stretcher and gently deposited the injured actor, face down onto the red blanket covering it. This was too much for the assailant who rushed to the stretcher and cuddled his mate. The scene was heartrending. The last I saw of the victim was his feet, pointing downwards protruding from the end of the stretcher. The usual small crowd of nosey bastards was waiting out on the street around the ambulance and police car. It is difficult to imagine what they thought when from the theatre emerged a laughing copper, two laughing ambulance men, and one prostrate man, on a stretcher, with a large lump in the blanket near his arse, screaming, 'Bastards . . . bastards'.

Chapter 4   Domestic and Public

IT could always be guaranteed that, during any normal eight hour tour of duty, police will be called to domestic disputes of some sort or another, at a ratio of about two domestics to every one other call. It is nice to know that the public will call police to try and solve their problems, but police training is very vague as to the manner of dealing with these disputes, particularly between husband and wife.

Things have to be pretty desperate for a woman to have to call a copper because of either assault, or fear of assault, from her old man. However it is not as simple as that. During my early days in the job I made the mistake of being a little heavy handed with any husband who, it was alleged, had just thrashed the living daylights out of his slight, five feet nothing, wife at their domestic abode. I soon learned, the hard way, just how far to go. Tread one inch beyond armed neutrality, show too much aggression towards the man, and his spouse immediately turns against you, and may even back up any complaint from her husband as to your attitude. This is painfully true and it is a lesson that some young coppers learn too late.

I can recall that only on very few occasions was I, as a police officer, called for by the husband. I answered one such call on a Saturday morning, where a member of the public dialled 999 after having seen a man leaning out of his window pleading with passers-by to call the police, on his behalf. I went to the house, knocked on the door, and there, as the front door opened, stood a violent Amazon, breathing fire. Her husband, the instigator of my visit gazed fearfully over her shoulder, black of eye and red of face!

'What do you want?' she snarled.

'We've been called to a disturbance here,' I replied, looking hopefully at the husband, who chose not to reply.

'Well mate, you can just piss off, I'm the one causing the disturbance here and it's none of your bleeding business, this is between me and him,' pointing over her shoulder at the man.

He shrugged his shoulders and backed away, his fright apparent. She folded her arms which were like hams, across her majestic bosom, pushed her chin forward, breathed heavily and shouted, 'Piss off and mind your own business!'

I wasn't going to put up with this sort of behaviour from any woman, so I responded as any red blooded man would have done, I decided to mind my own business and I pissed off as directed!

Next to domestic disputes, the greatest pain in the arse for the average copper, is the street demonstration. No matter what cause the worthies were supporting by marching, the faces were nearly all the same. The one exception was probably the anti-abortion law demonstrations. On these occasions one group was missing: The Gay Liberation Front. Their banner always caused me to hoot inwardly. Most banners have wind slits cut into them to allow the wind to pass through the banner and minimise the sail effect, this makes the banner carrying less arduous. The Gay Front did not have slits in their banner, they had a hole punched in the 'O' of the word 'Front'. Maybe Freud could have made something of this, or perhaps I just have a dirty mind, but I never saw it without smiling inwardly.

Without any doubt, the hardest of all demos to police were the National Front marches. The ferocity with which the Communists and Fascists dealt with one another was quite terrifying. I sometimes felt that the police cordon should withdraw, then surround both factions in one area and let them sort one another out.

But no, we could not withdraw, and were always placed in unprotected lines between the two factions. This meant that rent-a-mob left, and rent-a-mob right, were now going to war against the Old Bill. Blood was inevitably spilled. The aggressors used sticks, spit, contraceptives filled with urine, ammonia, sharpened pennies, ball bearings, boots and fists, usually intended for their opponents, but, in fact always striking the police cordon. There was always a mighty punch up. Hundreds of coppers were injured as many demonstrators were hurt and some budding 'martyrs' arrested.

We knew that we, the police, would eventually and at much cost, control the situation. Then, surprise, surprise, after it was all over there would be much hysterical discussion, some of it wise, all of it hindsight. It would eventually be decided, by the media, that it was the fault of the racist police, who were really responsible for the entire débâcle. Then there would be a flood of complaints.

I sometimes got a little angry during these demonstrations, particularly when someone took a kick at my wedding tackle. I invariably tried to smite them mightily, knowing that I would be shown to be a brutal copper, a lackey of the establishment, attacking a hairy underpriviledged representative of the working class. It would be forgotten that the hairy was probably a very privileged university student, and that I was definitely working hard for my pennies! I and my like would be maligned, and, if the worst came to the worst I could eventually appear before various inquiry and discipline boards and would be in fear as to my future livelihood. Always completely lost from view would be the fact that, had I not acted as I did, I would probably have ended up with three Adam's apples, two of which would have been my testicles, displaced by an underprivileged pair of boots!

Political organisations, particularly of the extreme left, ascribe political motives to coppers on these demos, assuming a political sophistication in the average copper that is just not there. I agree that the average copper leans to the right, but at demonstrations it is not right or left that matters, but right or wrong! The copper's prime concern is the defence of those items of his anatomy that are supremely important to him.

Coppers, at times like these, are an amazing lot. Some really are pigs, some are hiding behind a blue uniform and membership of a large organisation, but the vast majority are bloody marvellous *men*. They carry a steel plate inside their heads which they draw down, between them and memory, to forget the nasty side of life which they meet daily at their work. The front side of this steel plate reveals very humorous men, with tremendous knowledge of the vagaries of human behaviour and in particular of the inherent cruelty of man towards man.

Under pressure they are brave and confident, with the tremendous esprit necessary to help keep one another sane and well. If this is bad, then it is my kind of badness, and I was happy and proud to be counted amongst them. There are coppers who are sadists and power happy, but they lead a fairly lonely existence in the job. They are usually ambitious men and some gain promotion and disappear into executive offices away from danger. This is good for the public, though not so good for the coppers under their command. There are some good governors, however the oddballs amongst them are well to the rear when the chips are down, and blood is being spilled, whether this is happening in some lonely street in the small hours, or at a violent demonstration. When the dust has settled, these ambitious men, with an eye to their advance-ment and not the job, creep from the rear echelons to ask, 'Why, where, what and when?'

That the police of this country maintain a very high standard in their dealings with the general public is in spite of, and not because of, the standard of supervision and foresight they receive. The left is winning the battle to undermine the public confidence in the police service because the higher echelons of the service are staffed by the ambitious element of the job, who want to keep their noses clean for the next step in the ladder of promotion, and for that reason will not argue on behalf of the coppers they are supposed to lead! There are only two coppers I can remember in positions of authority in whom this quality is not obvious, and for whom I have some respect, Robert Mark and the present incumbent, Metropoli-tan Police Commissioner, Sir Kenneth Newman.

As a copper I have often laughed at the chanting, hairy, rent-a-crowd faction. Now they frighten me. They have successfully, over the past 10 years out-manoeuvred the senior officers of most police forces. The blunt sword of 'No comment' or 'The matter is sub judice' have failed to support the copper on the street who has been the fall guy every time. The stress of non-retaliation because of the superiority of the lefties' propaganda has caused many coppers to say to themselves 'Sod it, let them get on with it.'

The press camera will always catch the copper's fist flying through the air at the face of an innocent demonstrator, and seldom, if ever, will it record the moment before when the same copper had been kicked in the balls. The average reporter will emphasise, in his story anything that is sensational, irrespective as to right or wrong. The only time I have honestly known full support for the police in a public order situation was right at the beginning in the original Grosvenor Square anti-Viet Nam riots. That was only because outnumbered police dealt with the situation so bravely and at so high a cost, that it was impossible to do other than praise them. The lefties never made the mistake of putting police in so attractive a light ever again.

I will always remember attending a demonstration at Southall, after the Blair Peach episode. It was organised by the left and resulted in a large number of Asians marching through the streets of Southall. They had every right to do so, and would probably have done it without the organisation of the left. I was there. I suddenly saw small numbers of organisers urging the Asians to make the clenched fist salute as they marched past the spot where Peach was killed. This the Asians did. It occurred to me, that here were thousands of small businessmen to whom Communism would be the last ally in their money-making endeavours, who were the epitome of private enterprise, being brainwashed through emotion into parading their clenched fists. Sure enough, the following day, in the newspapers, and not just the *Socialist Worker*, but papers of varying political slants, were photographs of thousands of Asians, apparently supporting the Communist left, another ethnic minority turning away from the ugly face of capitalism, when, in fact, most were small businessmen emotionally blackmailed into a propaganda exercise on behalf of the portion of society directly opposed to their way of gathering capital. The Asians' fists should have been clenched with anger rather than in salute, for they were being used for political purposes and didn't realise it!

Chapter 5   Night Duty

THREE o'clock in the morning, breakfast finished, and patrolling, waiting for the dawn and then off to bed. No one can ever appreciate bedtime as much as a night worker going home. I used to listen to the alarm clocks buzzing away as I passed homes and think to myself, 'Get up you bastard, I'm going to bed.' Not this night though. A radio call to a house in the poorer part of my patch. The call was to a 'disturbance.' The title 'disturbance' covered a multitude of sins, from murder to a neighbour hitting a kid. It usually meant that the officer receiving the original call couldn't put a label on it, and left the blokes dealing with it unaware as to what they were about to deal with.

I arrived outside the address to find an ambulance sitting there, blue light flashing, the crew not in attendance. The front door of the house nearest the ambulance was ajar. I knocked on the door.

'Come in mate,' the gruff voice was that of a shirt-sleeved ambulance man.

'What have we got?' I asked as I entered the house.

'A nutter. She's in the garden,' said the ambulance man, pointing towards the rear of the house.

I walked through the house followed by two crewmen from the ambulance and a rather anxious looking West Indian, middle-aged and pyjama-clad.

'It's my wife, she has gone crazy,' the West Indian tapped his forehead with his finger.

As I walked tentatively into the back garden I heard the squeal of brakes from the road outside, obviously another police vehicle had responded. I was pleased to hear it. After the brightness of the house I waited a while for my eyes to focus in the gloom. I could see that the garden was surrounded by a brick wall about four feet high. At the end of the garden, which was uncultivated and debris strewn, standing on the wall, was an extremely large black woman aged about 50. As I walked down the garden path I accidentally kicked a can. The woman turned towards me and began gibbering in West

Indian dialect so pronounced that I could not understand a word of it. Of considerably more interest than her conversation was the fact that both of her hands were full. She was gripping, in her right hand, a small pickaxe and in her left hand a very large chamber pot. As I drew closer I heard footsteps behind me and saw, to my relief, two shirtsleeved coppers enter the garden.

The ambulance man called out: 'She's completely gone mate, she goes berserk if you get near her, so watch out.'

He then retired into the kitchen and I heard the chink of a tea cup and saucer.

I explained to the two coppers who had joined me that my intention was to get as near to her as I could and then try and push her off the wall. At which time we would all leap on her and try to restrain her. Every copper will tell you that anyone who has gone round the twist is capable of phenomenal feats of strength, and for that reason surprise was essential.

While they stood in front of her and tried to engage her in conversation I crept up to, and then on to, the wall about 10 feet from her. She was gibbering at the two coppers and waving the pickaxe about. I crept closer to her along the wall, deciding that I would concentrate on her right hand and the pickaxe. She was fully engaged in shouting at the two coppers as I suddenly launched myself towards her, confident that I could push her off balance and into the garden. As I did so she turned with remarkable speed and as I groped towards the pickaxe, I saw the pisspot, being propelled by a black arm like a side of beef swinging in my direction.

The next thing I heard was the raucous sound of a two-tone horn. I could hear the sound of laughter, it was the ambulance man calling in on his radio.

'We've got a PC coming in,' he hooted, 'knocked out by a woman with a pisspot.'

I realised that I was lying down firmly wrapped in a red blanket. My head hurt, and as I reached up to touch the tender spot I encountered a large dressing firmly bandaged to my head.

I opened my eyes and there in the ambulance with me was one ambulance man and a copper. Both were grinning.

'Fancy, a pisspot!' this from the grinning copper. I closed my eyes, the humiliation already sweeping over me. I could hear the conversation in the police canteen the next day . . . 'Have you heard about Brady, some bird laid him out with a pisspot. . . .'

And so, once again off to St Mary's Hospital, casualty wing.

Upon my arrival at the hospital the news had obviously spread that I was the copper whose head injuries had been caused by a pisspot. I was attended by nurses who were grinning and not at all sympathetic. In fact, like the lady with the pot they were all taking the piss. After a cursory examination by the casualty quack, I was packed off to a ward for the night. Unfortunately Gigs was at this time not in too good a state of health and certainly not well enough to attend the hospital to visit her woe-begotten husband, whose head was aching and who was in dire need of some sympathy.

My two sons, Mike and Alan, were brought by police car to the hospital. As I saw their white faces peer around the ward entrance I was filled with considerable affection for them. Mike was about 15 and Alan about 12 years of age at the time. If they knew the cause of my discomfort they did not grin, for which I was grateful. It made me think how difficult life can be for coppers' kids. People tend to work off their antagonisms on them at times of stress. Equally difficult is that they are expected, by their contemporaries, to be holier than thou because their old man is a bogey. Sure as eggs are eggs if they do try a little bit of naughtiness with their mates, around the corner will come dad in his police car, they are never free from him and it is unfair. It is little wonder that police children sometimes go off the rails. It is a wonder that it doesn't happen more often, they have to bear pressures on occasions that they don't even understand. The anxiety of the dad that his kids should reflect his pristine image, is sometimes too much for his children and both society and father must take the blame.

Neither of my lads have joined the police force. I have always sung the praises of the force at home and tried to offer

mitigation for those evil bent coppers who have sullied the
name. But I am glad they haven't followed the old man's
footsteps. Times have changed and the bogey is always to
blame and is always wrong; why should my kids slog away at
law enforcement? Besides, had they joined the police they
may have ended up as senior officers and that shame would
have been too much for me!

Chapter 6   George Davis was Innocent?

ONE of the perks of being both an experienced copper and
also an advanced driver is a 'Q' car posting. The 'Q' car is an
unmarked high powered police car, with a plain clothes crew.
The word 'Q' was derived after seemingly harmless merchant
ships in the first world war, which were in actual fact armed
auxiliaries to the fleet, and were called 'Q' boats. The 'Q' car
was not supposed to be like a police car at all, and the crews
were not chosen for their academic distinctions.

The work was extremely pleasurable. To be able to
concentrate on criminal activities, to be able to forget
constabulary dignity and scratch one's arse in public, was
indeed a pleasure and a welcome break from routine
coppering. The vehicle and crew were completely crime
orientated. It was rewarding because it was devoted to, in my
mind, the most important part of policing . . . nicking villains.

The car to which I was posted was coded Yankee One One.
It covered a large area and was superimposed on existing
police coverage for that area. I remembered sadly attending,
many years before, the funerals of the crew of Foxtrot One
One, a 'Q' car, whose crew had died in a tragic shooting. It was
during the manhunt for a man named Roberts, one of the men
wanted for the murders, that I had first carried a revolver on
police duty. However, those thoughts were far from my mind
when I joined the crew for our first tour of duty. The sergeant
was Jock Lawie, with Keith Brewin as the CID aide. I was the
driver. The tour turned out to be a good one with plenty of
arrests and excitement coming our way. We were a lucky
crew, and a happy one. Jock was a dour Scotsman, his sense of
humour was very deep and only became apparent when one
got to know him well. Straight as a die and a good copper.
Keith was a very happy man, his idea of bliss was to be in a
pub, with a pint in his hand and surrounded by crumpet. He
always smelled 'nice' and took considerable verbal badinage
for the pongs which emanated from him in the close confines
of the car. Keith was a pleasure to be with, but I knew the

quiet sergeant better, having served at the same station with
him for some years.

There was nothing special about that day: at first. It was fine
and clear. As we tumbled into the car and prepared for the
eight hours patrol, we were oblivious of the events that were to
follow, and were to cause us much trouble and considerable
notoriety. This day we had an additional passenger, a
detective constable from Edmonton. He had been working on
a job in which a load of Scotch had been hi-jacked from a lorry
on his patch. As the result of a little grassing from an
informant, it had been learned that a baker's roundsman in the
East End was flogging bottles from the stolen load, whilst on
his round. Making a little extra 'bread' was the remark made,
which caused groans all round. The three litre Vauxhall we
were using had, according to the crew, sufficient power to
overhaul a baker's van; they weren't so sure about my ability
to catch the bloody thing! The search warrant was checked and
off we went, with a waft of aftershave from Keith and a
mumbled Scottish obscenity from Jock. We were going to turn
over the bakery and see what transpired.

Going away from our own patch on inquiries was always a
welcome break and we were full of high spirits in anticipation
of a successful trip as the information was from a good snout
who had been productive in the past. Our radio was switched
off, we had booked off for inquiries. Repartee began. We
discussed the coital capabilities of passing crumpet, whether
or not Keith had had his end away the night before, and who
was responsible for the last fart, which had almost caused us to
abandon the car in the middle of the road. I was completely
lost and relying on the crew to direct me to our destination. All
was well with the world and we were completely relaxed.

We drove steadily up to a road junction in East London.
Suddenly there came, from our right, the squeal of tyres and
the raucous blare of a police two-tone horn. In our car instant
alertness, the transformation from complete relaxation that is
the hallmark of the professional policeman. Across our bows
at a very fast speed, considering the state of the vehicle, tore
an old battered Ford Zephyr. It contained four men, looking

very heavy indeed. 'Heavy' in police parlance means extremely villainous. Three of them were wearing motor cycle crash helmets. The fourth bareheaded. A respectable distance behind and making a lot of noise, was a police Rover, headlights blazing, blue light flashing. As he crossed in front of us the police horn was wailing like a banshee.

'Bugger me, look at that!' Jock came to life. He was wasting his breath, we were already looking hard. I spun the wheel and accelerated after them.

'Switch on the set,' said Jock to himself, as he leaned forward and pressed the switch. The powerful car surged forward, the adrenalin started to flow again. A warm glow of excitement filled the car. You could almost taste the atmosphere, this was what it was all about. The radio was going berserk. Apparently whilst we had been toddling along, all hell had been let loose. There had been an armed robbery at an East End electricity office, where the wages had been lifted by the blokes we were chasing. It had become apparent now as to why the police car in front of us was a respectable distance from the bandit car. Not only were the villains armed, but they had just shot a copper.

The bandits' car was all over the road, but there was absolutely no way that it was going to escape from the police cars up its arse. The villains' driver was doing very well under the circumstances, but I wondered why he had chosen such an old banger for the getaway. It was only later that I discovered that this was a hi-jacked vehicle and that things had gone wrong for them, right from the beginning of their escapade.

We were third in the queue at this stage, first the bandit car, then a police Rover and us. But I knew we had enough engine to overtake the bandit car and try to have him off the road when the chance arose.

'Shall we have the bastard off the road?' I shouted to the crew.

Immediate acquiescence from the occupants. I was about to give the Vauxhall full bore when my heroics evaporated, like piss on a warm pavement. Suddenly the rear windscreen of the Zephyr shattered outwards in a thousand pieces, and, not for the first time in my life, I saw the flash of a gun being fired in my direction. I say, in my direction, because, even should you be one of thousands and someone fires a gun in your general direction, you always feel that he is firing at you personally. As the shotgun blasted off, the blue light on the roof of the police car ahead of us was blown apart, and out of the corner of my eye I saw the front offside hubcap of our car sail through the air, like a discus, about five feet from the ground, travelling hard and fast!

The scene continued to unfold before us like all the police movies we had seen in the past. The police car in front of us was weaving all over the road, just as we were. The villains were letting off the occasional blast from their shotguns to keep us at a respectable distance.

As we ploughed through fairly dense traffic, I glanced in my mirror and saw that behind us he had a stream of police cars, a mass of blazing lights and blaring horns, cutting through civvy cars abandoned by their drivers left, right and centre.

The radio was still going berserk, with shouts from various operators combined with static and background noises. The calm voice of the operator in the Information Room at Scotland Yard was trying to bring order to the radio transmissions, but to little avail. All this noise, the exhortations from my own crew, coupled with the occasional blasts of gunfire which was interposed with foul expletives from both myself and the crew, increased the excitement. I was concentrating on the driving, envying the luxury of the racing driver who has no one coming the other way.

I narrowly missed a Mini, the driver of which, I am sure, would never be the same again, as he slewed across the road, then 'We've got the bastards!' shouted the others. I saw exactly what they meant. There, ahead of us was a dual carriageway leading to a large roundabout (Charlie Brown's Roundabout). The traffic ahead of us was solidly blocked and the villains' car, followed by half the Metropolitan Police, was hurtling towards the traffic jam like a kamikazi closing on the deck of an American aircraft carrier. Whoops of delight issued from the radio loudspeakers. There was absolutely nowhere for the villains to go! It was fast approaching crunch time.

One of the most highly qualified members of any robbery team, is their driver, the 'wheelman.' This wheelman certainly knew his stuff. Drivers recruited for this sort of caper were a special breed. Apart from the obvious driving skills, they required a ruthlessness and disregard for anyone else, the ability, to, coldbloodedly, run down anyone who got in their way. He was no exception. He performed a four wheel drift on to the grass verge running alongside the nearside of the road. We, of course, followed. The fox was going quite well, but it looked good for the hounds! None of us, at that stage, took into account that the foxes were very well armed and more than willing to shoot. Such is the excitement of the chase that thoughts like that are blocked from the copper's mind.

Skidding and sliding on the grass verge, with absolutely no chance of stopping dead on such a surface, the procession noisily sped on past the nearside of the stationary cars in the roadway. The motorists, some of whom had got out of their cars to see what all the fuss was about, scrambled frantically back into the safety of British Leyland with considerable alacrity.

'That is definitely their lot,' said a voice in the back of the car. Directly ahead of us was a maze of scaffolding holding up a temporary advertising hoarding, it completely blocked the grass verge. Alongside it a mass of cars, closely jammed together. No room! Again the wheelman, in the pursued car, earned his money for that day. He slewed his car to the offside and headed bare arsed towards the solid mass of cars with a burst of shotgun fire at police cars.

The Zephyr tore through the stopped cars pushing them out of the way but leaving a gap for us to follow. Then with a crash followed by the inevitable tinkle of glass, the front of the car embedded itself into the fence of the central reservation.

'They're bailing out!' At least that message came clearly across the RT.

They were indeed bailing out. The confusion was unbeliev- able; screams from the female occupants of badly damaged cars, the shouting of coppers, people darting in all directions: the civilians away from the chaos and the blue clad figures towards the eye of the storm. I pushed open the door of our police car and ran towards the villains' crashed car as fast as my rather plump body could carry me. That car was now hidden by other traffic, including a very large lorry.

I skidded on foot round the large lorry. This must be it now, I would soon have my first view, at close hand, of the actual blokes who had been behaving in such an unsociable manner. What I then saw curbed my enthusiasm and caused both Jock and I to slide to a halt. It felt like a Tom and Jerry cartoon, where the body is still travelling forward, and the legs are frantically reversing like mad!

A large American car had been stopped on the other side of the central barrier. It was facing the direction from which we had just hurtled. A fattish man, without a hat, was running towards the far door of the yank car.

'Remember him' I thought to myself.

'Remember him, look at his face, remember him.'

'Watch him, watch him, remember his face Dave,' I said to myself again and again.

Then puzzlement. Why have I stopped, why have I screamed to a halt, why don't I get after them?

I took a sharp intake of breath, a mixture of emotions swept over me . . . anger . . . fear . . . frustration, for, once again I was peering down the barrel of a gun, again the bore looked like the Mersey Tunnel. This time, for a change, it was a revolver, a different kettle of fish to a shotgun. With this fellow the weapon was being held very professionally, a double hand grip, arms straight, this bloke really did know what he was doing. He looked like a spaceman, dark visored helmet and green overalls. He was tall and thin. I peered hard, trying desparately to see his face, to remember if I could, as clearly as I had the plump man before, but it was to no avail. I couldn't make out the features of the guy with the gun at all.

One thing I was sure of, that by his crouched attitude and aggressive stance, coupled with the fact that this lot had already shot a copper, I knew that I would never get to him without losing the ninth life. What about all the unarmed combat I had learned about in the Marines and in the police? On this occasion all of that training came to a load of bollocks. One move and kaput, very annoying, but nevertheless true. If only Doyle or Bodie had been there it would have been all right. I cursed the rules and regulations that politicians had formulated that put police officers in this situation. If only one of those smug politicians who criticize from the safety of the television studio could have been there.

The man with the pistol gestured for Jock and I to get down. I half knelt, half sprawled, with Jock beside me doing the same . . . still no chance. I cannot remember having ever been so frustrated and angry in my life. He backed away towards the American car, now containing all of his mates. As the gun moved further away it was possible to encompass a larger part of the local scenery.

The hypnotic gaze at the muzzle of the gun became less urgent. I saw, further down the road, a copper. In shirtsleeves and hatless, he was dashing about commandeering cars and vans, and then driving them across the road in an attempt to block the route of the hi-jacked American car. The copper obviously knew, as well as we did, that armed police were on the way and if Fatty, and his mates, could be forced to abandon the car and make their way on foot, they would be eminently nickable.

Robbers are extremely brave when they are armed, until they find an armed copper in front of them. They tend to wilt a little under those circumstances. The odds are suddenly all wrong and they usually pack it in. The road, by now, was almost blocked, the shirtsleeved copper having worked like a beaver. A small, one vehicle, gap was all that remained. He ran towards a transit van on the verge. His intentions were obvious, it would be the last piece of the jig-saw, the barrier would be complete once it was in position. The American car, now fully loaded, the spaceman with the pistol having leaped aboard, roared off towards the last gap in the barrier. I jumped to my feet, brave again now that we were safe from the pistol.

By the time we had climbed the barrier we had already lost the battle even if we hadn't lost the war, and I shouted with frustration as they tore away. I remembered all the films I had seen where Robin Hood got away and the Sheriffs' men were laughed at, in their frustration, by an unsympathetic audience.

Still I remembered one of the men's faces, it was imprinted on my mind, and I knew that if ever I saw him again I would know him.

To my horror the villains' recently hi-jacked car did not immediately head for the remaining gap, but towards the brave, shirtsleeved copper. His attention was focused on the last remaining vehicle with which he was going to complete the road block. I could see what was about to occur and attempted to shout a warning, but it was too late. The escaping car accelerated violently and the front of the car collected the policeman in its path. He was scooped up onto the bonnet, up the windscreen and over on to the roof of the American car, his arms and legs waving loosely. With a swerve and a scream from the engine the car leapt forward again. For a brief second of time the copper was poised on the roof and then he was thrown on to the roadway. He ricocheted against the side of the van he was attempting to use to close the barrier. He lay inert and only his hair waved gently in the slight breeze.

'Christ, he's dead,' I thought, 'he can't have survived that, the bastards!' The face of the fat man sat securely in my mind. It would, I was certain, stay firmly in my mind until, one day, I was sure I would see him again and rest my hand on his shoulder. The hi-jacked car disappeared into the distance, travelling very fast. With all the police cars, including mine, on the wrong side of the barrier. The only slight consolation was that the money, the proceeds of the robbery, was still sitting in the abandoned car against the central barrier.

We gathered together back at the 'Q' Car. The injured copper was whipped away in an ambulance. Back to the local nick in response to a radio message, where we were shown some photographs of the actual robbery taken on the spur of the moment at the scene. They were, as far as I could see, useless. Taken at a distance and unrecognisable. I was sick, but knew I would recognise the fellow with the paunch.

Some time later, many days in fact, I was on duty at my own station when I was warned to attend Walthamstow nick for an identity parade. (Incidentally, and as an anti-climax, we had, after leaving the nick and looking at the photographs, continued our journey and nicked somebody for the stolen whiskey, but it was a poor substitute for losing the robbers earlier.)

On arrival at Walthamstow Police Station I was told, by a uniform inspector, that an identification parade was about to be held in connection with the armed robbery. If I saw anyone on the identity parade who was concerned in the incident I was to place my hand on his shoulder. I had not been concerned in any of the inquiries that had been made but still I knew that if 'paunchy' was there, I would most certainly recognise him. I was taken to the station yard and there was a line of men. As I passed through the door and into the yard and walked towards the line, I glanced along the assembly and there, to my intense pleasure, was the man with the paunch. I walked along the line. I had to be sure, there was no way that I was going to make an identification unless I was absolutely certain. I stopped in front of him. My mind went back to the day of the robbery; I looked at him carefully. I was so sure that, without delay I reached out and rested my hand on his shoulder.

This man was George Davis. He became a *cause célèbre* and in time to come was to cause me considerable distress.

Time passed until I attended Walthamstow Magistrates' Court to give evidence as to the circumstances of that day of robbery and my subsequent identification of George at Walthamstow nick. I saw, at a distance, Rose Davis, his wife. As time progressed I admired her tremendously for her loyalty to her husband, though of course, I disagreed with her assessment of the situation, which was that George was stitched up and was not involved.

At long last, and some months later at Number One Court at the Old Bailey I spent a considerable time in the witness box. The only surprise was that George seemed to have lost a bit of weight. I related my evidence under great pressure; it was suggested that I was very much mistaken and that it wasn't George I had seen on the fateful day. I was sure I was right. At the end of the trial the other three men in the dock were found not guilty, but George was convicted and sentenced to 20 years for the armed robbery.

As far as I was concerned the matter was over and justice had been done. How wrong I was! I was sad to see a man being tucked away for such a long time, but I remembered the poor copper who had been run over, and the second copper who had been shot by the villains.

Some months later I arrived for duty at Hornsey nick and heard that the Yorkshire cricket pitch had been dug up during an interesting stage of a Test Match against Australia. I wasn't overly upset about it until I discovered that this was apparently the start of a campaign, the slogan of which was, 'George Davis is innocent, OK?'

The slogan began to appear on walls all over the East End. It was an area I very rarely went to, but when I did, the number of signs surprised me. This was followed by numerous events in support of George, including the ramming of the gates of Buckingham Palace, as a gesture against the wrongful conviction of an allegedly innocent man.

The campaign grew to such huge proportions that the majority of the police, public and politicians, began to believe the allegations. A large number of ordinary members of the public supported the campaign. It was obvious that I and the other officers involved were going to be under suspicion. I knew that I was not mistaken. It hurt even more when various coppers approached me and whispered conspiratorially, 'Did you stitch George up Dave?'

If they didn't believe me, then what chance did I stand?

The basis of the argument became apparent when, on a TV current affairs programme, I again saw Rose Davis allege that George was a simple minicab driver and that armed robbery was definitely not his scene. Locally, people were not too aware of my connection with the case. Whilst sitting having a quiet pint I could hear folk discussing the case. The vast majority seemed to side with George and thought that he had been framed. I, of course, had to stay quiet and swallow both my beer and the natural urge to defend myself.

The power of the media was such that I suffered a great deal mentally, but the more I remembered the day of the robbery the more convinced I was that I was right. Nobody, but nobody, is infallible, but I was convinced. The campaign increased in its intensity. It got to the stage that when a television programme started a typical media presentation of the case, indicating that the evil police had created yet another injustice, I just had to leave the room.

My family stood by me at home, but it hurt that my sons might even, under the constant barrage of propaganda, believe that their old man had lied.

A slightly more sinister aspect inserted itself into the situation, when, on a number of occasions I became aware that I was being followed. It may have been that anxiety and stress had got hold of me, but I had done enough trailing to know when it was happening to me. Was it the Old Bill, or the villains' lot? To this day I don't know. I think it was probably the job keeping an eye on me, but for what? Protection or surveillance?

I continued my duties and time progressed, until, one day whilst out patrolling in the police car, I was called, by radio, and instructed to return forthwith to Hornsey Police Station. I asked the reason and no one seemed to be able to tell me. I arrived at the station office and without a word being said I was escorted to a small office on the CID floor. Inside were two men, both obviously senior police officers. Their demeanour was far from friendly so whatever it was, it wasn't to tell me that I had won the pools.

They introduced themselves as a detective superintendent and detective chief inspector from the Hertfordshire Constabulary. They told me that they had been deputed to investigate the George Davis case. The complaints and campaign had now become official. I was relieved, at last I could have my say after the months of enforced silence, but it wasn't going to be quite like that. They informed me that complaints had been

received as to the identification and conviction of George
Davis for armed robbery. I felt like a villain in their presence;
they were workmanlike and distant. The notebooks were
open, pens poised, and the interrogation commenced. For the
first time in my career I was on the wrong side of the desk, and
I didn't like it much.

How I wish that the public, who moan about how the
investigations of complaints against the police are handled,
could have been present on that day. I was interviewed as to
the events that had led up to the case at court. The
interviewing was handled aggressively and it was obvious to
me that the attitude of the investigating officers was to find any
crack in my recollection of events and then promptly tear me
up for arse paper! I was quite angry in my mind. I was a police
officer who had done his job to the best of his ability, and here
I was, deeply in the shit, and being treated much worse than
any villain. The advantage I would have had, had I been a
villain, would have been the presence of a solicitor, to protect
me. No such luxury exists for a police officer under these
circumstances. The only warning I received was the statutory,
'You are not obliged to say anything unless you wish to do so
etc.,' How often had I recited that formula in the past, to
criminals, whilst interrogating them, and how uncomfortable
it was to be on the receiving end. Particularly when, to my
mind all that I had done was the duty for which the public paid
me!

Throughout I was adamant that every portion of my
evidence had been made in good faith, but with continuous
aggressive questioning my internal anger increased. I was
completely honest in my replies to them, I had no fear of being
tripped up, because I knew I was telling the truth as I had seen
it. After four hours the interview was terminated, I left the
station and continued on my patrol. I was extremely tired and
angry. I hoped that the incident would not adversely affect my
future attitude to police work . . . It did not!

There were a further three bouts of interrogation, of equal
length and intensity as the first, over a period of some months.

Then months of silence. It was constantly pointed out to me that George was a simple minicab driver and was not, or ever had been, an armed robber. I became desperate, but no one believed me, or at least, very few. From that day on, I heard nothing from anyone as to how the investigation was going, and was left in a nervous hiatus of uncertainty. No comforting or disparaging word, absolute silence. I was almost mental hospital material!

Home, in our Hornsey flat, life continued as usual, with, by now, only the rare mention of the Davis affair. I continued to work from Hornsey Police Station, and the snide comments about 'stitch up' began to subside. Back home one evening after late duty, I settled to watch a little TV the phone rang. I lifted the receiver, 'You stitching bastard, you won't get away with it, keep looking over your shoulder.'

The gruff voice stopped, there was a brief moment and then the receiver was replaced at the other end. I felt awful, not because of the implied threats, but because, at last, the job had reached out and encompassed my home and family. I was absolutely confident that I could deal with most police situations, but this unnerved me quite a lot.

The phone calls continued for some time, and, eventually I reported them to the investigating chief superintendent from Hertfordshire. Coincidentally it was at about this time that the calls stopped. I didn't have any idea as to the caller's identity but his attempts to unnerve me were very successful. My bottle hadn't gone, but it was rocking about a little on its base!

Time passed, it was a beautiful day, I was, as always, patrolling in my police car. As I passed a newspaper seller on the High Road a placard caught my eye, I thought I saw the name George Davis. I retraced my steps. I was right, I had. There it was, stencilled in deep black—

GEORGE DAVIS RELEASED

I couldn't believe it. I quickly bought a paper. It revealed that though George had not been pardoned, he had been released because of possible doubts about the current law on identification, and that changes in the law were to be established as regards identification in the future. I was extremely surprised to find that the only emotion I felt was that of relief because now my ordeal would be over.

The only sadness that I felt, was that now the general public would be convinced that George was just a minicab driver and not a robber. They would also believe that the police, and that included me, had stitched him up. Still, it was over at last. I felt happy for Rose, his wife, she had kept faith in her husband, had worked like a trojan and campaigned vigorously, with no holds barred, for his release.

Photographs appeared in the press as he left prison. He was pictured on his way home with one of the Krays. Although, as far as I knew, there was no connection between them, I was pleased to see George in such company. George then quietly faded away into the background, and I settled into routine coppering, with another lesson learned.

Came the summer, we were as usual, not too flush, so Gigs and I decided that we would see the sights of London and behave as tourists do, rather than go away for the break. This we did, and we thoroughly enjoyed ourselves visiting the various landmarks. I collected a mild bollocking from a copper in the Houses of Parliament, whilst passing through, for sitting down on one of the front bench seats in the chamber. I deserved it and scooted out somewhat redfaced, with Gigs following and laughing like a drain at my discomfiture. We wandered from the House of Commons, and strolled through Parliament Square.

Suddenly, in the distance, coming from the direction of Whitehall, I could hear voices chanting. A small procession entered the square. I saw that they were carrying banners and shouting. They were accompanied by a small squad of coppers. The banners declared boldly, 'Free George Ince.' It was obviously a campaign following the apparently successful George Davis campaign. I stood with Gigs, and watched as they passed. There were about 20 to 25 men and women in the group. Suddenly, startled, I saw a face I recognised, it was Rose Davis. Her eyes were shining and her face wreathed in happiness. I had only ever seen her before either angry or distressed, and wondered at her unrestricted delight.

Then all became clear, strolling beside her in the afternoon sun, was, George Davis! I watched him with the fascination of a rabbit faced by a stoat, there was something different about him. I puzzled for a moment, with a smile I realised that the slim George Davis of Number One Court, Old Bailey, had got himself a beer gut. In fact he was positively plump! My mind went back to the robbery and suddenly I felt so much better. I pointed this out to Gigs and all she did was to squeeze my hand. I was anxious not to be spotted as any subsequent disturbance would have been horrible with Gigs present. We crept quietly away; the quiet pint we had later has never tasted so good.

The tale ends as I was sitting one day in the Collator's Office at Hornsey, perusing a list of wanted villains before I went on patrol, when the phone rang. The collator placed his hand over the handset and said, 'It's for you Dave, it's Holloway nick.'

The voice at the other end sounded loud and happy, 'We've just had an armed blagging at the Bank of Cyprus, on Seven Sisters Road.'

'So what?' I replied

'Well Dave, we thought you would be interested to know who we've nicked red-handed . . . your old mate Georgie Davis!'

'*The* George Davis?' I held my breath.

'Yes.'

I hung up. I sat back and heaved a sigh. The months of tension dropped away. It proved nothing with regard to the first robbery, but, by God, it indicated that perhaps George was not just a simple minicab driver after all!

One bottle of whiskey and all was well with the world.

No one has ever since alleged a frame up. The media was extremely unrepentant about its previous attitude towards police and the words 'George Davis is innocent, OK?' have faded from the walls of the East End. Only George knows the truth, I only know what I believe to be the truth. Who knows whether I would still be under investigation now, if George had been a simple minicab driver and not an armed robber. . . .

Publisher's note.

On March 18, 1975, George Davis was sentenced to 20 years' imprisonment for his part in an armed robbery on the London Electricty Board, in Ilford. (The robbery and some of the incidents surrounding it formed part of the plot for the *Law And Order* series on BBC television.)

On May 11, 1976, he was released from prison on the Home Secretary's recommendation of the exercise of the Royal Perogative. Roy Jenkins, the Home Secretary, gave as the reason for the recommendation 'the weak evidence of identification' and made it clear that there was no evidence suggesting that Davis was innocent.

On July 24, 1978, George Davis was sentenced to 15 years' imprisonment for his part in an armed robbery in Seven Sisters Road. The robbery was photographed by a *Daily Express* camera team which was in position before the robbery took place; Davis and other men were arrested at the scene by detectives who were waiting in ambush.

Chapter 7   Voodoo

THE teeming population of Hornsey was a complete cross-section of the old British Commonwealth, West Indians, Cypriots and various African nationals. They each had their fair share of honest men and villains. Without doubt, though generalisations are always dangerous, the most cunning, the smoothest talkers, the men with the best business acumen, were the immigrants from Nigeria.

Their requests for police intervention almost always occurred over some dubious financial transaction, where they had, allegedly either failed to pay a bill, or were not in receipt of a debt owed to them. So you can imagine my surprise, when, after receiving one particular emergency call from a frantic group of Nigerians, I discovered that no financial transaction was involved whatsoever.

I arrived at a shabby terraced house, in a shabby street. Inside all was chaos. the house seemed to contain most of the ex-inhabitants of a Nigerian village, who had come to the UK to make their respective fortunes.

A bevy of fairly unattractive females surrounded me, all verging on the hysterical. I was ushered noisily into a downstairs room. They pointed to a quite attractive girl in her early twenties. Her black cheeks glistened with tears. Her eyes were wide and staring and her swathes of colourful clothing much dishevelled. There was not a male in sight.

After some screaming confusion I was able to find out what was wrong from an old crone whose voice and vocabulary outshone the others. It appeared that the young Nigerian girl, now somewhat calmer, was much fancied by the male occupant of an upstairs room at the address. He was a businessman . . . weren't they all? He had made many approaches in the past week, so I was told, for sexual favours from the pretty girl. All of which, she stated, she had spurned!

That very afternoon, so it was alleged, whilst the girl was sitting quietly in her room, the businessman had burst in. The story continued with much wailing and gnashing of teeth. He was carrying a six-inch nail, bent into a 'U' shape and wound in coloured wool. He also carried a stick of wood about two feet in length, to which were glued portions of chicken feathers and chips of coloured glass.

At this stage of the tale my mind boggled, was I about to hear something original? I was! The girl was told by the man that the articles were voodoo. This information terrified her. It was, allegedly, further explained to her that the stick was to ensure that, what he was about to do to her, would protect her from pregnancy. Then, to her terror and amazement, he pushed the stick up her skirt, and gently brushed it against that portion of her anatomy, in which, at the time, he had considerable interest.

The final threat made to the bemused young lady, was, that if she refused him, the voodoo metal would leap from his hands and tear her assunder in the same spot!

By now, the lass, being in considerable terror, immediately decided that what he had to offer her was infinitely preferable to the voodoo instruments, and had, albeit reluctantly, allowed the evil Nigerian gentleman to have his way.

'What a load of old rubbish,' I thought to myself, my European mind refusing to accept such an incredible tale. Like a typical male under these circumstances, I honestly felt that the bird had closed her eyes and thought of Nigeria, after having succumbed to the blandishments of the man, and, as sometimes happens, had had a touch of the seconds. She must have concocted this ridiculous story as a saver, in case of unwanted pregnancy.

However, it had to be investigated, anything was possible. Where is the man now?' I said to the wizzened old girl, she seemed to be the boss lady.

She shrieked and headed for the stairs. As she did so, all the other ladies present started wailing and also dashed for the stairs.

As I was almost trampled to death in the rush, I thought it would be a good idea to get to the alleged rapist first. It was obvious that if I didn't, I would probably be the first British copper to witness a ritual tribal castration, and I felt that any admission from the gentleman would lose some of its veracity, if, at the time of the admission, he had, just been deprived of his balls! Lawyers are a dreadfully distrustful lot where the police are concerned. It would probably be alleged, at the end of the day, that I was the castrator.

I could picture the scene at court, the lawyer wagging his finger at me, 'I put it to you, officer, that in order to obtain a confession from the defendant, you forcibly deprived him of his manhood. That you castrated this unfortunate coloured man, partially to obtain a confession and partly because of your insane hatred of ethnic minorities resident in this country.'

The jury, naïve and understanding, nodding in agreement, as the large, fat officer in the witness box, a personification of police brutality, struggled to avoid the gaze of the poor innocent coloured man, unjustly treated and sacrificed on the altar of racism. . . .

I forced my way up the stairs and past the frenzied female mob. I mounted the stairs to find the man who had mounted the unwilling female. At the top I turned towards the sea of black shining faces and shouted at the top of my voice. They stopped and stared, somewhat apprehensively at this screaming nutter in blue.

I opened the door at the top of the stairs, and there, understandably terrified, was a dapper, well dressed, middle-aged Nigerian. I closed the door behind me.

'Can you hear them?'

'Yes sir,' he trembled.

'What's this all about?'

His confidence grew visibly before my eyes as he realized that I was prepared to discuss the situation. Now was his opportunity to impress me with the fact that he was an extremely decent chap and not a voodoo rapist, as alleged. In cultured tones he informed me that the young girl had pestered him, unmercifully, for sex, until, at last, being a mere mortal, he had succumbed to her obvious charms. Then, to his horror, his eyes widened at the memory, she had, at the culmination of the act, made those stupid and malicious allegations.

I was fairly impressed with his demeanour, which was in direct contrast to the hysterical outrage of the women outside. Whilst I was nodding in sympathetic approval of the helplessness of men against the vile cunning of the female, my gaze wandered round the small bed sitter. I noticed that one of the drawers of the cheap dressing table was not fully closed, a portion of clothing was dangling from the gap. This completely out of character with the remainder of his immaculately kept room.

I strolled across the room towards the dressing table, his voice faltered, anxiety oozed from every pore.

'Dear, oh dear,' I thought, 'His bottle's gone!'

As I opened the drawer, his voice droned to silence in mid sentence. There, looking up at me from an assortment of clothing was a bent nail, wound with coloured wool, and a stick with chicken feathers and glass fragments adhering to it. I looked at the items for some time. Then, with eyebrows raised, transferred my attention to the nice Nigerian gentleman, with, what I hoped, was a look that said, 'You lying bastard!'

His hands were facing upwards, his arms spread, his eyes wide and frightened. Without saying a word he was pleading guilty! I walked across to him, smiled and said softly, 'You are nicked!'

He immediately burst into tears and sat back on his bed. There was no way that I could get him, unharmed, past the viragos on the stairs, not in one piece, that was for sure. I had no wish to lose whatever one could lose in these circumstances trying to get the cunning sod out of the house. A quick radio message and reinforcements arrived; we all wended our weary way to the nick.

It was back to Grace, the Nigerian lady from the canteen. She was her usual outspoken and noisy self, with no respect for authority. She had goosed the dignity out of many a senior officer who had made the mistake of turning his back on her; she was beloved by every copper who had crossed her path. She fiercely defended 'My boys,' against all criticism, no matter from whence it came.

I decided to check the authenticity of the voodoo items allegedly used in the rape. Watched by countless constabulary eyes, all in on my little game, I sauntered into the canteen.

'Hello Brady,' Grace smirked, poised to do me a mischief at the slightest opportunity.

'Watchya Grace, how about a bunk up then?'

I placed the woollen-clad nail and the piece of wood on the counter, completely forgetting where they had been in the not too distant past, and careless as to the culinary flavour it may add to the coppers' sandwiches. Grace looked down at the articles, her eyes widened slightly and she fled from the canteen. I chased, and somewhat shamefacedly caught her. Grace almost never ever forgave me for the incident. It did however reinforce the argument that the little Nigerian bird had possibly been truly had over, and I was quite ashamed of my initial reaction to the complaint. Rape should always be dealt with by a woman, not a fat lout of a copper with a distorted sense of humour!

Chapter 8   Against Women

I HAVE always felt that the Sex Discrimination Act should not apply to the police service. I do not feel that it is sexist to want to ensure that the violence of modern criminality is not directed at women, the vast majority of whom do not have the physical strength to enforce the law in a violent situation without the assistance and protection of male officers. This is a biological reality which all the equal rights legislators should bear in mind. Every policewoman who is injured on duty is not only a victim of the villains, but of the legislators and of the women who demand sex equality no matter in what sphere. More and more women police will be killed and injured in the future and society will be doubly sympathetic to them and their kind. I am not a chauvanist and firmly believe that there should be equal rights for women, but I don't feel that these rights should extend to the right to be maimed.

I do not approve of women in the front line of the police service. They are as out of place as women soldiers would be in the front line of the army in wartime. There is a war taking place on our streets 24 hours a day between police and criminals and the physical requirement required for dealing with vicious criminals, is honestly beyond most, though not all, of our serving policewomen's capabilities. They may not admit this, but I am sure that most of them are aware of it.

The average woman copper on the street survives the physical trials and tribulations of police active service through the cossetting and helpful care she receives from the male officers with whom she works.

They are infinitely superior to their male counterparts, in dealing with women and young persons. They are considerably more adept at sorting out rape allegations than unsympathetic male officers. I admire intensely the work done by women police in their proper fields, but it is an unfair burden to a street officer, to lumber him with a female to take care of at times of physical stress and danger.

The senior ranks of women in the police service, are now, because of integration, actually commanding operational units at station level. They tend to be extremely knowledgeable book-wise and law-wise, and inclined to overstate their authority. But if it were left to the women in the police to arrest vicious felons, then Dartmoor and other prisons would be empty. The woman copper on the streets is in the same jeopardy as her male counterparts. Basically they are a pleasant dedicated crowd and very likeable, and in the non-physical requirements of ther job are equal if not better than most of their male colleagues. They are rightly very defensive if any insinuation is made about their ability as police officers.

I have a lot of very good mates amongst women police officers with whom I have served and my opinion will displease them. It is about time somebody said what is truly in the minds of male police officers; they can't say it, perhaps I can on their behalf. I am being realistic and not bowing to public opinion initiated by the equal rights lobby. I believe in equal rights, I also believe that it is the overall stronger physically male, who should be responsible for the safety of women in a situation where the women may be in some danger. There is one thing that most men can do better than most women, and that is to fight on behalf of society, the physical battle for order on the streets.

To the angry lady coppers, and there will be many, I would say you do so well those parts of the job that women should specialise in, but please, leave the sharp end, on the street, to male officers who can then concentrate, on the restoration of order, rather than having to first worry about the safety of the policewomen accompanying them. If a woman is, and many are, better than me at a specific task, then I am not going to get up tight and see it as a slur on my human rights, so why should feminists go berserk if I say that the average man is stronger than the average woman, physically? The police are society's strong right arm; too many women police will weaken that arm.

Chapter 9   Breaking Into Beans

SUNDAY afternoons were always a pain in the arse. Other people were not working and all was quieter than usual. It was three o'clock in the afternoon, and the prospect was of many hours of boredom before the pubs opened and the drunks started their evening's fighting. There was seldom much trouble when the pubs closed at Sunday lunchtime. The husbands seemed to want to rush home fairly promptly, for either Sunday lunch, or a bunk up, depending on how much drink they had consumed! The radio operator was quietly drowsing in the seat beside me. The Jaguar patrol car was performing nicely. All was peace and quiet, then out of the blue, a call for us. 'Yankee One, Yankee One from MP. The Broadway, Crouch End, Informant complains of unusual noises from unattended shop premises.' 'MP from Yankee One, your Message received,' from my operator, now awake.

We were about five minutes fast drive from The Broadway and the streets were virtually free of traffic, so I slipped the Jag into low gear for acceleration and sped quickly, but quietly, towards the Broadway. Never, never should police sound a two-tone horn when attending suspect calls, it would be akin to warning the villains that you were on your way. There was no adrenalin flow on this occasion, the possibility of this being a genuine call was practically nil. Most villains, and all prostitutes, seem to favour a six day week, I've never known why. Perhaps, like me, they object to working when everyone else is having a day off.

A few minutes later we cruised quietly up to the front of the shop. I had dropped my mate off on the corner to cover the back, just in case the call was genuine. I now remembered the shop as a cafe that had become unoccupied some weeks earlier. It was next door to a jewellers. In the window of the empty cafe was a sign indicating that shopfitting was taking place. Outside the shop stood another police car, belonging to the duty officer, who was obviously inside the premises dealing with the call.

In another shop some two hundred yards down the road, the

manager, working overtime on stocktaking, had just finished stacking a huge pyramid of tins of baked beans in his front window. The last tin, at the apex, was placed in position with a sigh of relief for a tedious job completed. Outside his shop was a parked Ford, unattended, for the owner had run out of petrol. In fact, the owner was, at that moment walking towards his car with a gallon of petrol in a can, clutched in his sweaty hand. He was immensely relieved to have found a garage open nearby and was looking forward to refilling the car and continuing on his way. Hope you've got all that.

Meanwhile I sat looking across and through the nearside window of my car, through the plateglass window and into the shop. The duty officer walked out of the front door, smiling.

'Beat you to it Dave,' he boasted, 'they are just shopfitters putting up shelves for the new owners.'

As he spoke, two overalled men, who were inside the shop, straightened up from the hole in the wall on which they were working, and looked out towards the street. The hole was in the wall adjoining the jewellers. The taller of the two looked a trifle startled as our eyes met, and rightly so! I recognised him at once as, not a shopfitter, but a fairly well-known shop-breaker. We had met in the past when I had felt his collar under somewhat similar circumstances. I was prepared, almost, to presume that he may have gone straight, but wasn't willing to accept such a hypothesis without a further little chat.

His mouth framed a slightly surprised 'Ooh' and he said something to his scruffy looking mate. As so often in police work the shit suddenly hit the fan. They dashed out of the shop, going like the clappers.

'Lovely,' I thought, 'a plea of guilty!'

They were off, like a prostitutes' drawers at the sight of a 10 pound note! As they reached the open door, the duty officer, who had his back to them, was completly bowled over in more ways than one.

One of them screamed off to the left, towards my mate on the corner, and my old customer took off to the right. The duty officer went off like a long dog after the first man, and was soon joined by my operator. They disappeared from view like a scene from the Keystone Cops. The other felon had run back down the road in the direction from which I had arrived. I was now faced with a little problem. Were I to stay in the car I would have to turn it round and waste time. If I were to get out I would still be wasting time. When pursuing a frightened villain the one thing a copper has not got, is time. I wonder how many Olympic sprint records have been broken, by a villain with a copper close up his arse. . . .

I looked over my shoulder; he had now obviously got his second wind and was running very, very fast and would soon be gone forever. I just had to catch him now, as he would surely swear mistaken identity, and also produce a dozen alibi witnesses if he were allowed to escape. I thrashed the car into reverse gear and screamed off after him, backwards. Every motorist will tell you that the most unstable vehicle in the world is one being driven very fast in reverse!

The manager of Victor Value's Store stepped back to admire his mathematically perfect pyramid of baked bean tins. The owner of the Ford drew nearer to his car, full of pleasurable anticipation, now that the unease about his lack of petrol had ended. The fleeing villain ran towards them both, breathing heavily over his exertions and anxiety about possible arrest . . . the thought of porridge does something to the breathing apparatus of the human body. Also in hot pursuit and heading towards them at a very high speed, backwards, in a Jaguar, was PC Brady, who was becoming incensed with the whole affair and rapidly developing a rear skid! A skid, whilst travelling in reverse, without a lot of recovery space, is a very difficult thing to deal with, and particularly unpleasant in a narrow road, with shops on both sides.

Just to round the situation off, the whole affair was also being witnessed by two Chinamen, from the window of the Chinese Restaurant which was directly opposite the pyramid of beans.

The villain, whom I shall now call Charlie, decided to cross the road, at speed, to get to a nearby corner, where, hopefully he would disappear from view for ever. As he crossed my stern

I knew that it was quite likely that I was about to flatten him with two ton of Jaguar. For one brief moment I was tempted, then thought of all the reports I would have to submit and the thought went away. I was already fighting to regain control of the vehicle and straighten the skid. He was the last straw. I slammed hard on my brakes and the Jaguar went completely berserk.

The Ford owner stood transfixed throughout, his eyes and brain concentrating on the black police Jaguar now hurtling, with very little, if any, control, towards his little car, his pride and joy.

The manager of Victor Value's staggered back from his bean mountain. He was somewhat frightened. As he looked past his collection of tins he could see the little Ford, and as he looked beyond the Ford, in a direct line he could see the hurtling police car, with a fat dervish at the wheel. He turned and ran, who could blame him!

Charlie, whose every instinct was to keep going, stopped at the sound of screeching tyres. He was breathing heavily and watching, with some pleasure, the impending demise of his pursuer.

I was, once again, deeply in the shit, hanging on like grim death to the steering wheel. I saw, out of the corner of my eye, two Chinamen. Chinamen? I knew I had been travelling far and fast, but not that fast surely? My back was firmly wedged into the seat and my arms were eight feet long. My eyes bulging like racing dogs' bollocks and my knuckles white with the tension of fright.

First the little Ford . . . craaash!

Then the shop window . . . craaash!

The about 10 million tins of beans . . . craaash!

My mind raced, my only salvation would be to nick Charlie. I leapt out of the bent police car, rocketing over tins of beans like an octopus on roller skates, out of the gap where the shop window used to be and out into the street. There was Charlie, open mouthed, forgetting to run in the ectasy of seeing his old adversary, Jaguar and all, disappearing from view through the broken window.

The manager of the shop, physically unscathed, appeared to be having some sort of fit. I was surprised that, as an apparent epileptic, he should hold such a responsible position. The Ford man was sitting on his petrol can. I think he might have been crying!

I bounded towards Charlie. I was red-faced and suffering somewhat from shock. I was also very angry. I had to collar the bastard, I had to. To capture a villain and whilst doing so, wreck a police car, was slightly excusable. To wreck the Jag and catch no bugger was a different kettle of fish. The powers that be would be quite cross anyway, particularly as they would have to pay for the Ford, the shop front and Victor Value's beans . . . plus convalescence for the manager.

Charlie suddenly emerged from his bliss and realised his danger. He turned away to have it on his toes again. He was obviously still quite knackered from his previous two hundred yards of exertion, and was also emotionally drained from the pleasure of the past few seconds. I was propelled by adrenalin and fear. He didn't have a chance. I grabbed him in a quick hammerlock and bar, and he was on his toes and hurting.

'Leave it out Mister Brady, I ain't going anywhere, and neither are you in that.' He nodded towards the shop window and giggled hysterically. 'You are fucking right,' I snarled in his ear. 'Look what you made me do.' I pointed to the chaotic collection of debris.

The manager was looking at us, he was wringing his hands. The Ford owner had thrown his can of petrol to the ground. He was looking at me and using language the like of which, for originality and venom I have never heard before or since. My mate and the duty officer came struggling back with Charlie's companion in tow. They both stopped and gazed in amazement at the scene before them. My mate, a man of full descriptive powers and a wide vocabulary, looked at the villain he was holding, who, in turn, looked back in to his eyes. Then together, as though rehearsed many times, they gasped in unison, 'Fuck me!'

Back to the nick with Charlie and his mate. Numerous patrol cars arrived on the scene to gloat over my misfortune.

Various senior officers snapped the cobwebs that bound them to their desks, and sauntered along, shaking their heads and clucking their tongues at the irresponsibility of the lower ranks, who caused so much unnecessary paper work.

Charlie later made a statement, which he signed, stating that it was only because of my superb driving that he was still alive which was very friendly of him under the circumstances. He almost felt that the subsequent porridge would be worth while, as he could regale all of his friends with the story of his nicking, and would, on release, earn many a free pint on the strength of it.

Chapter 10   Grit Your Teeth

SHOW me a dentist, and I will show you a devout coward. Dentists and heights are, to me, the epitomes of absolute terror. It is because of my reluctance to visit dentist that I probably still have my own teeth. Both fears are a legacy from my time in the Marines, where, as merciless instructors forced me to climb cliffs and swing from ropes. The only medical treatment I ever had in the Marines was from a Naval dentist. I hope times have changed as far as the Marines are concerned. I wish now, that when I had sat in his torture chair, I had reached out just before he started the treatment, and grasped him firmly by the testicles. I could then have looked up into his eyes and said, 'Now, we aren't going to hurt one another, are we?'

But this is only to explain what happened when I paraded for duty one night. As I settled in the car to start the night's patrol, a gentle pain twinged through one of my bottom teeth. I hoped fervently that it would go away. It did not. I suffered in silence for about 20 seconds and then started to complain. For the next three nights and days, I complained. The younger coppers could not understand my reluctance to visit the dentist, having tasted the delights of modern painless treatment. On the fourth day of my misery, smelling strongly of oil of cloves, with which I tried unsuccessfully to hold the ache at bay, I had now started day duty, and was sitting in the canteen, holding my jaw with one hand and reaching for the clove oil with the other. Ray Collett wandered casually into the canteen and sat nearby. I trusted him implicitly, but my trust was misplaced on this occasion.

With a crash the canteen door flew open and a phalanx of coppers raced into the canteen. My trusted friend Ray grabbed me from behind, I was floored by a blue swarm and felt handcuffs click my wrists together. I was lifted bodily and carried struggling out into the station yard. There, waiting, was the police van, its doors wide open, and another two coppers waiting, arms outstretched.

I was thrown into the van still fighting, but to no avail. I hadn't got a clue what was going on, but whatever it was, I didn't like it! As the van roared out of the station and along the road, the noise from it was deafening. I was shouting obscenities at my brother coppers, but was helpless in their grasp. The van stopped, the doors flew open. I immediately recognised the road as Weston Park. A number of passers-by stood, mouths agape, as the coppers dragged me out. I could see that I was outside the dentist's surgery, and there, waiting at the open front door was a large man in a white coat. He was laughing very loudly.

As it dawned on me that I was about to receive dental treatment, fear coursed through me, and I started to fight again. Along the corridor into a surgery. I was forced into the chair handcuffed to the arm. Unbeknown to me, the blokes had become completely fed up with my performance over the past few days, plus the fact that the nick and all the cars stunk of oil of cloves. Ray had visited the dentist, an Australian with a sense of humour, and explained the situation. The dentist was quite happy that I should be dragged to the surgery, but had made it plan to Ray that he would only perform treatment with my permission once they had got me there. To my shame I surrendered completely; surrounded by grinning faces, including the dentist's, how could I let them see that my bottle had definitely gone?

The Aussie treated my tooth, and the bastard didn't hurt me at all! If he had done so, then my long period of suffering would have been worthwhile. As it was I left the chair quietly after treatment.

'That wasn't so bad,' said the dentist, 'was it?' I agreed. I don't know what all the fuss was about. Dentists hold no fear for me now. Have I visited a dentist's since? Not bloody likely!

Chapter 11   The Knifeman Cometh

LEAVE days were very few and far between, and all the more relished because of their infrequency. Gigs was bustling about the flat. She never sat still for a moment longer than was absolutely necessary, being as much addicted to work as I was to my job.

'Dave, can you give me a hand with the shopping today? My back is playing me up a bit.'

If Gigs complained of any pain or hurt, she was really in trouble. I am sure that were she to be run over by a bus and you were to ask her how she was, she would reply, 'Fine thanks.'

For that reason I willingly agreed to accompany her to Crouch End, our local shopping centre. If I had known what the morning was to bring, then I'd have stayed at home!

We made our way towards the shops, which were within walking distance. Having been a policeman locally for about 20 years, I knew a fair number of people, and rarely, if ever, was a journey with Gigs undisturbed. She could read a situation like a book. Various people with sundry reasons used to stop us and chat. Gigs had, over the years, developed a nose for what was going on. A request for advice she would deal with by just standing with me, but not joining in. The more furtive approach from one of my ex-customers would cause her to wander casually on and then wait patiently, just out of earshot, so as not to inhibit the erstwhile informant from dropping someone deeply in the shit. The things she saw and knew, about the folk in Crouch End was unbelievable, and yet, to her eternal credit not once did she in any shape or form, indicate her knowledge. A rare creature, a woman who could be trusted absolutely with a secret, either knowingly or inadvertently, and would keep it a secret.

On this morning we met our usual quota and slowly worked our way towards the shops. A final chat with Jim, the paperman on the corner by the bank, before visiting various shops, with Gigs spending and me waiting outside to take over the load in my pretty shopping bag.

The last port of call was Dunn's the bakers, where I stood scratching my arse, figuratively, whilst Gigs was inside. A very large Negro about six feet three inches in height, sauntered past me, heading towards the Natwest Bank on the opposite side of the Broadway. It would be wrong to describe him as furtive, villains rarely are, but I recognised that he was working hard at not being furtive. My nose twitched. That indescribable copper's instinct took over. He was such a big bugger, that when Gigs appeared with various cakes and sausage rolls, I was happy to dismiss him from my mind.

'Sod it, it's my day off . . .'

'That's it then,' said Gigs, 'we'll go home now.'

We strolled back towards the clock tower, nattering away and at peace with the world.

Suddenly a shout, the words indecipherable, but carrying a mixture of rage and fright in their intonation. I looked around, back towards the bank. Through the fairly heavy traffic and in the middle of the road, was the big black sod I had seen passing Dunn's. Outside the bank, just struggling to his feet, was a middle-aged Indian man. He was obviously distressed and was shouting and pointing to the mobile mountain trundling my way. I saw that the villain was carrying a Natwest cashbag, bulging with what one could reasonably assume was money. He had obviously just blagged the Indian at the bank.

'Oh Christ,' I thought, 'here we go again.'

A second look and my enthusiasm waned a trifle, for in his free hand he was wielding a long bladed knife. He must have called the knife Moses, because everyone was opening up before him life the Red Sea.

I remember thinking, in the brief time available, that he was so big and obviously strong, he was going to take some stopping, but with the additional insurance of the large knife the bugger was home and dry. Then, as had happened to me on so many occasions in the past, I was committed to the situation and poking my nose in through pure instinct. Over 50 years old and well past my prime, with not many active years of coppering to go, I was definitely not suited to a prolonged struggle with a four foot coward, let alone a large and fit man.

Still, there it was, my fat body, horizontal about three feet from the ground. Shit, I was doing a rugby tackle. Never done one of those before . . . should be interesting.

'I'll look a right prick if I miss him . . .' floated through my mind.

I saw two moving, jean clad, tree trunks before my eyes and took a frantic grab at them. They tumbled over, with my 15 stones wrapped around them. As he hit the roadway the vibration was unbelievable. I clung desparately too him as he half struggled to his feet.

'Police,' I gasped, as though those magic words would cause his immediate surrender. His reply was a large black fist, the size of an elephant's testicle, blacking out my vision, smoting me mightily in the region of my right ear. I was like a tuning fork, the blow vibrating me all the way down to my toes. He continued to clobber me, all around the same area of right ear. I began to wilt somewhat . . . bash . . . bash . . . bash! 'It's a good job he's hitting me on the head,' I thought, 'otherwise he'd be hurting me.'

I tried the magic formula, 'police officer,' again but little good it did me. He clouted away even harder. By clinging around his legs, my position was such that I could not reach him to retaliate. I did not want to let go and possibly lose the bugger, so I hung on as he clouted away even harder. I was lapsing into semi-conciousness, aware of Gig's voice calling. I noted the large crowd of curious onlookers, some male and large, with the hearts of mice. Suddenly the blows ceased, thank Christ! I saw a man who looked like a copper in plain clothes, move in on us. The villain's hand swung, a flash of reflected light from the knife followed by a flood of crimson as he chopped at the chin of my brave friend, whoever he was. I began to climb up the legs I was grasping and as I did so the three of us were in fond embrace.

Down to the ground we tumbled. As our black friend at last fell down with his face to the road, I found myself at his shoulders. The back of his curly haired head was towards me; I grabbed his ears, one in each hand. I glanced across to my helper, a very brave bloke indeed. His face was bloodied and his chin was hanging off. 'Are you in the job?' I gasped.

He nodded, spraying blood all over my newish jacket. He was Detective Inspector Marvin, better known as Lee, of course. I had never met him before. He was on his way to work when he spotted my dilemma.

The distant sound of police horns grew steadily nearer. I knew that at least one of the onlookers had found the courage to phone the Old Bill. I felt quite angry with the man on the road beneath me. I made the quaint discovery that every time he struggled to get free, he could be quite easily discouraged by a rapid wriggle of his ears. This caused his flat nose to rub violently on the tarmacadam. In fact in my bemused state I may have even given him the occasional wriggle even when he didn't struggle . . . quite a few wriggles in fact! The Old Bill arrived in a flurry of blue. The van doors were flung open and my recent assailant disappeared inside, hustled there by the local coppers whom I knew well, including, would you believe, my old mate Ryan David. How the van shook when our villain was inside. The fool must have started to fight again.

Chapter 12   Jokers in the Pack

ONE would presume, from various writing, including mine, that police work is a succession of continuous exciting incidents and drama. It is not! The job can be tremendously boring. But it is bearable in that it is interspersed with moments, and they are are usually brief, of acute activity, horror, fear or hilarity! The possibility of activity around the next corner holds back the boredom. Life at the sharp end of the force is one that calls for tremendous *esprit* and a strong sense of humour. The humour may seem to be, on occasions, childish, and is nearly always barbed and to an outsider apparently cruel. It helps to dispel the despair, occasioned by the insights which events offer, as to man's inhumanity to man. In a report commissioned by David McNee (the former Metropolitan Police Commissioner) that showed the police in a 'warts and all' light, it was indicated that police tended to like a little drink. So would you. As you stroll off to work, think how you would feel if, as the day unfolded, you untangled a mutilated heap of flesh from the remains of a motor car; soothed a weeping daughter to whom you had just broken the news that her mum was dead; broke into a house at the behest of neighbours, and there stumbled across the maggot ridden remains of a poor old man, who had died some days before, fought, with some desperation, a drunken lout, whose idea of a good time, was to terrorize his family; to be subsequently facing an inquiry, as to why you used too much force to separate him from his family, which he was physically assaulting at the time, with that inquiry taking place at the behest of the family you had saved! Wouldn't you fancy a drink at the end of the day? Wouldn't your humorous escapades verge on the hysterical? Of course they would!

I have seen policemen, almost beside themselves with delight, hiding behind a tombstone in a cemetery near the nick, in the early hours of the morning, waiting for the new probationary constable to pass that way en route to his beat, groan and moan loudly as the poor lad passes, and then fall about clutching their stomachs, as white faced, he gallops off into the night. I have taken part in drink ups, off duty, when contraceptives full of beer have hurtled across the pub, bursting on impact. Childish? Of course, Release from tension? Definitely.

A past master at the art of creating chaos in the police canteen was a good friend of mine, Jimmie French. A slight man for a copper, he had a diabolical sense of humour. This humour was not always appreciated by the wives of the policemen whose ties he had cut in half. Whilst visiting my home, for a gathering of coppers and families, he removed the lavatory handle from the cistern early in the proceedings, which caused some consternation to subsequent drunken users. When remonstrations were made to him regarding the handle, he denied emphatically any part in the theft. He did however promise to make good the loss before the morning, He did. When, the next morning I was leaving home to go on duty, I opened the front door and an entire lavatory system including pan, pipes, cistern and chain fell into the front hall. They were very old and cobwebbed. The pan was far from hygienic and the smell unpleasant. I was hysterical with amusement; not so Gigs, who instructed me, in no uncertain manner, to dispose of the objects. Have you ever faced the task of disposing with an entire lavatory system?

Grace, our Nigerian canteen lady, always entered whole-heartedly into the canteen high jinks. She always was extremely noisy and, if irate, would chase us from the canteen wielding a large knife. I think that, without doubt, our moment of greatest triumph was when two officers from the then newly formed Community Relations Department, visited the nick. They called into the canteen, impeccably dressed in civilian clothes and bearing the statutory Scotland Yard briefcases. The canteen was fairly crowded, and as I sat near the two men, whose sole function in life was to foster racial awareness in the force, I winked and nodded at Grace. Her large white teeth beamed from her black face. As the men sipped their teas and mumbled together, I suddenly stood up and shouted,

'You black cow, this grub is 'orrible, you'd better bugger off back to Nigeria where you belong.'

'Don't you call me a black cow, you honky bastard,' screamed Grace. She scrambled over the counter and headed hot-foot in my direction, her face contorted with rage.

There was a moment's stunned silence. The troops there, who knew just what was going to happen, sat still and waited. Grace was leaping about as though demented. We both shouted racial slogans at one another. The community relations men sat for a brief moment, unbelieving and horrified, cups poised. Then, as one, they raced for the canteen door, struggled a little as they became jammed together, and disappeared. Grace and I fell into each others amrs, helpless with laughter. Her eyes were shining, the tears clearly visible running down her cheeks. Suddenly the door opened and in rushed one of the two men, grabbed his forgotten briefcase, and then, slightly pale around the gills, shot out again. It was too much, Grace and I now verged on hysteria. I waited for a message to kindly attend the chief superintendent's office, but it never came. Fortunately.

Chapter 13   Marooned

FINSBURY Park is a large park situated a stone's throw (by a fairly strong athlete!) from Arsenal's football ground at Highbury. It has every amenity that a London park situated smack in the centre of a fairly deprived area should have. The area surrounding it is primarily occupied by Greek and Turkish Cypriots, and West Indians. It has wide stretches of browny green sward, football goal-posts, dingy trees, prostitutes, layabouts, muggers and furtive pimps, loitering and waiting for their toms or prostitutes to appear with the money earned after each transaction.

At dusk each day the park is locked, and the undesirables drift out into Seven Sisters Road, where they continue to ply their various activities into the small hours of the morning. The park contained the usual cafe and pavilion. The toilets were havens for homosexuals, and whatever sympathy one may have had for their plight, was quickly eroded by the sordid, unsavoury urine scented, shabby surroundings in which they were forced to operate. What was a constant source of amazement to me was, that the vast majority of these unfortunate and sometimes unpleasant men were persons of some financial substance, mostly middle-aged, well dressed and well spoken.

Apart from the usual patrols in the area, the park was occasionally visited by police during the night hours whilst it was locked. In the centre of the park was a large boating lake with a small overgrown island at its centre. This island was the home of two very large birds, cranes I think, though I am not sure. Not only were they huge, but they were also very dishevelled and the wickedest bastards you would ever wish to meet. How they got there, or why, I was never able to discover. But, at night, there was never any doubt about their vicious temper.

To enter the park at night we had a key to one of the gates, and it was our practice, when all was quiet, to congregate the night duty relief at the lakeside. Many was the police cadet who was launched into the lake in a dustbin and pushed from the side to float in the bin, which, almost without fail, drifted to the centre of the lake and then overturned, depositing its unfortunate occupant into the smelly dank depths of the water.

I remember, with some satisfaction, a particularly obnoxious copper, whom I shall refer to as Smith. He had just arrived from the training school and was, even more than usual, full of his own piss and importance. All young coppers, including myself, go through that phase, and it is important to pass that period of your service as soon as possible. It is often cured by a punch in the mouth from a drunk.

However this particular lad, Smith, was big, young and fit. It was felt that any personal attempt to inhibit his ego, would be fraught with a high degree of physical risk.

'Come on down to the park,' I said to him in the small hours of a cold Autumn morning.

'Why?' he said, not in the least suspicious.

'Well we always meet there with the other lads for a smoke and a natter.'

He agreed.

We arrived, and, as usual, the place was fairly alive with coppers. The park-keeper, who was friendly towards police, was, at this time fast asleep in his little bed, but had lent the keys to the boathouse to 'his lads' as he always referred to the Old Bill. With a triumphant shout the metal boat was hauled out. With the exception of the lad maintaining a listening watch on the radio, we all piled aboard, with our new man, Smith, perched in the bows. An imperceptible nod, we rowed towards the island wooping and singing loudly, to annoy any possible occupant on the island . . . Smith, in his innocence joined in with wild abandon.

As we ground ashore, a hand pressed firmly into Smith's back and he rolled onto the bank. Frantic backpaddling rushed the boat away from the island, and we floated and waited some 30 yards from the bank. Smith, somewhat muddied clambered to his feet, shook his fist and shouted,

'What's the bleeding game?'

We made no reply and he shook himself and with a

contemptuous leer turned his back on us and disappeared into
the undergrowth, swaggering slightly to indicate that he didn't
give a monkey's. We waited in breathless anticipation.
Nothing, silence, what had gone wrong? Suddenly all was
well; a hideous shriek rent the air. I had been expecting it but
it still frightened the life out of me, so what had it done to poor
old Smithy?

Crashing and thundering noises issued from the island. The
fluttering of heavy wings, the shriek of the birds, crashing
undergrowth, and muffled squawks emanating from a human
being in great terror. Then Smith appeared, dishevelled and
scared witless.

'For fuck's sake help! Come and get me off!' His high
pitched scream was as from a woman in labour.

From the warm darkness a cacophony of voices called,
'Bollocks!' and 'Swim you bastard.'

Roars of laughter which paled to gasps of terror as, from the
undergrowth behind Smith, appeared two evil heads with long
beaks at the end of arched angry necks. With wings flailing and
beaks pointed they burst out on to the bank, very, very angry.
Smith arched into the air, his arms and legs windmilling, and
plopped straight into the filthy depths of Finsbury Park lake.
After a short delay he emerged with greeny slime oozing from
every angle and aperture of his body. He shook his fist, 'You
baaaarstards . . . you baaaarstards!'

We rowed rapidly for the shore, fast, with Smith, no mean
swimmer, in hot and angry pursuit. Sobbing with laughter we
finally reached the shore. Smith, now exhausted, dragged
himself from the smelly pool and lay gasping on the bank.

To ease his torment we comforted him and suggested that in
future, if he promised to reform, we would allow him to join
with us in dealing with the next super ego to emerge from
Hendon training school. He wasn't too much trouble from
there on in.

Chapter 14   Low Profile

SINCE the advent of the Race Relations Act and various legislation to protect the ethnic minorities, a new phrase has crept into police vocabularies . . . 'Low Profile Policing.' What it really means is that senior officers, in deference to misguided opinion from the vociferous and influential far left, decide because of possible adverse publicity, or because police have insufficient strength on the ground, to opt out when any situation becomes politically dicey.

This approach becomes clear at the initial briefing for a specific operation. Phrases creep into the pre-operation briefing such as, 'Don't be took keen to nick them; a nick for a minor offence is hardly worth a riot.' Or, 'You'll be sitting down a side street in coaches. Remain in the coaches no matter what you may hear over the radio, unless you are called.'

There was such a situation in Finsbury Park during a bank holiday in August not too long ago. For some years we had been involved in the Notting Hill Carnival. It always started as very jolly and interracial. Coppers were photographed with black women, who were nearly always sporting the copper's helmet. All smiles and racial integration. What a different story when darkness fell. Out would come the muggers, in force, and running battles would ensue between police and villains, for villains they were, irrespective of colour. As this was taking place in the Notting Hill area the vast majority of the villains involved were black. Therefore in the eyes of the media it ceased to be cops and robbers, but was elevated into much more newsworthy scene of the fascist police versus the oppressed minority.

These bank holiday high jinks spread to several metropolitan areas, and in particular to Finsbury Park, with its large West Indian contingent. At bank holidays the fair in Finsbury Park used to operate for the enjoyment of the masses. In 1977 and 1978 the fair developed and degenerated into the usual fracas, with shops looted and people, both black and white, assaulted and robbed. Then, with the 1979 fair looming ahead, I heard, for the first time, the magic words, 'low profile.'

We arrived at Finsbury Park and debussed at the park keeper's lodge in the centre of the park, hidden by trees and bushes from the fair. Coppers en mass are a blasé lot and there was considerable conjecture that this new 'low profile' was going to be a wash out and absolutely impossible to apply.

The fair was crowded and bustling, with tinny music wafting through the air, and the glare of fairground lights, attempting to liven up the squalor of the dismal area. The vast majority of the crowds were coloured families genuinely enjoying themselves. Among the joyful assembly were groups of 10 to 20 teenage youths, most of them unemployable rather than unemployed. This condition would have occasioned some sympathy, were it not for the arrogance with which they treated their own mature population. They gathered in groups in the fairground, surly, and tense.

Among the large crowds patrolled eight coppers in pairs. They had been carefully instructed to antagonise no one, whatever the provocation, but the local shopkeepers had boarded up their shop fronts hours before. Gradually the groups of coloured youths began to merge in the centre of the fairground. The majority of them wore large, brightly coloured, woollen caps, as the caps gathered together a huge bright blast of colour took over the centre of the area. It was only then that it was realised just how many of them were in the park. They numbered, by now, about two hundred.

A gentle movement stirred the crowd. It was like cattle in an old western movie immediately prior to the stampede. Radios crackled as the experienced police officers patrolling reported their suspicions to their seniors. I was there and was aware that a show of force, at this time, in the open space of the fairground, would probably nip whatever was about to happen in the bud, and would discourage those faint hearts among the assembled hats. Better a battle ground of our own choosing, if battle there was going to be.

But no, the coach loads of coppers, out of sight, sat immobile. The springs were coiled, ready to go, all that it required was a finger to pull the trigger. Just to disembark and show themselves would probably deter the majority of the assembled, brightly garbed youths from violent and unlawful activity. However the spring remained coiled and the trigger unpulled.

Suddenly, with no given word of command, a roar and off the mob went. The two hundred rapidly growing as the fainthearted joined them. They swept through the park towards the busy centre in Seven Sisters Road. The eight coppers were brushed aside and the former peaceful crowd had become converted to a knife and club wielding horde. As they poured through the park gates and out into the street, the familiar mob sounds of breaking glass and screaming women could be heard.

I picked myself up from the ground and sent a situation report over my radio. Still the trigger was not pulled. Groaning people, mostly coloured, littered the area through which the mob had passed. Black and white families with crying children and angry fathers. The afternoon's pleasure had become, for them, a nightmare. Meanwhile the coppers sat in their coaches . . . angry . . . low profile!

The swirling, excited mob spilled into the busy street. Robberies, some violent, were being committed there and then. The misery being caused to the innocent can't possibly be assessed. At long last the radios began their string of orders to various units. I was aware that there were ample police to restore order but suddenly realised, to my dismay, that all that was happening was that cordons were being established at various locations to contain the mob in a given area, with strict instructions not to go in and stop the lawlessness.

I found myself, with about 40 other policemen, strung across the entrance to Blackstock Road. In the distance I could see other cordons in Seven Sisters Road and Stroud Green Road. The mob was indeed penned in, but in a busy area within which it could do untold damage to people and property. There we stood, the mob tearing the place to pieces. Bottles were being hurled and were arcing from the mob into police lines. The occasional copper was carried away. The

trigger had indeed been pulled, but the bossmen had left the
safety catch applied!

I was in the cordon with some young but very good coppers,
men with a generation of policing ahead of them, whilst I was
heading towards the end of my service. The cordon was loudly
voicing its opinion, 10 minutes of police work and it would all
be over. Wandering about the cordon were a number of senior
officers. The big brass were there to ensure that the policy laid
down would be applied, come what may. Their brown gloves,
distinguished air and complete disregard for the unfortunates
caught up in the mob made me seethe with rage.

Then, to our collective horror, we realised that behind the
mob we were facing, was a Bingo Hall, and issuing from the
hall were hundreds of middle-aged women and men. They
were leaving after their evening's harmless entertainment.
These people were, unknowingly, moving straight into the
area controlled by the mob, with the mob between them and
the police.

I remember calling out to a senior officer of the danger these
people were in, and being told, 'Stand your ground, stay
where you are.'

The unsuspecting bingo players began to enter the edge of
the mob. An old man suddenly threw his arms into the air and
fell down. By his flailing arms it was obvious that he was at the
least, being assaulted, and at the worst, robbed. As I saw the
old boy go down I joined a chorus of disbelieving shouts from
the police cordon,

'There is a man being robbed there!'

We pointed, and as the other coppers saw this we started
across the road to rescue the old boy and arrest the robbers.

'Get back, stand your ground.' This, loudly, from a much
braided senior officer.

I approached the officer, and said, 'This is disgusting,
people are being robbed and hurt over there and we are
standing here watching it!' I felt a terrible shame sweep over
me. I later discovered that the man who had been robbed had
in the course of the robbery, lost the sight of one eye.

Still the cordons stood still. I thought I knew why the senior officers had adopted the attitude in spite of seeing what was going on. With the minimum of police activity under provocation, there would be less criticism in the next day's press, but at what a terrible cost. I had always thought that if an offence was being committed, no matter by whom, be it a Member of Parliament or a tramp, then, as a police officer I would proceed against the offender, no matter what the odds. I had always, through my service acted thus and often suffered accordingly if the odds were not right. Perhaps, I thought, I was behind the times; political influences had intruded into the realms of straightforward policing. Sod politics, every person has the right to expect a policeman to intervene on his behalf if he is being unlawfully treated, and 'low profile' is a direct negation of this principle.

At last, the mobs grew tired and were allowed to disperse quietly through the cordons. They had had a lovely time, and because of low profile would be back again next year!

To indicate the political attitudes to policing, I remember, at a Crown Court, during a trial after a demonstration at which I was involved in the arrest of a man for assaulting a police officer with a lump of wood, that my political motives were questioned. The defence barrister, defending the alleged Communist being charged, apparently noticed the Korean campaign ribbon on my uniform jacket, asked, 'Officer, did you serve in Korea?'

'Yes Sir,' I replied.

'Did you shoot any Communists whilst you were there?' the brief smirked.

'Yes Sir,' I again answered.

'Did you volunteer to serve in Korea?'

'I was a regular Marine, I went where I was sent.'

The brief paused, happy at apparently having established that I was anti-Communist, having served in Korea and had arrested his client with my anti-red hat on. Nothing at all to do with a copper being clobbered on the head with a lump of wood during the demonstration.

The judge looked towards me, 'Officer,' he said, 'Did you serve in Europe at all during the war?'

I replied in the affirmative.

'Did you instigate any activity against Fascists at that time?'

'I did, your honour.'

The judge glanced at the defence brief with a raised eyebrow. The brief scowled and I received no further questions on that tack.

My position as a copper at a demonstration is aptly illustrated by remembering the conversation at that court. Politics don't matter a monkey's. It's not Right or Left, it's merely right or wrong that counts. One other aspect of 'low profile' that concerns me is the attitude of the press in the reporting of so called racial riots. I have been on duty at riots where robberies have occurred, and damage inflicted on a fairly large scale. To my surprise the press and television have indicated satisfaction as to the limited scale of the carnage. I wonder, could it be that 'low profile' now extends to the media? Do they fear copy-cat riots as have occurred in the past? Low profile is an insidious disease which is creeping through society. It is a 'perhaps it will go away if we leave it alone' attitude. Instead it is weakness which offers an attractive temporary placebo, but which is very dangerous for society in the long term!

Chapter 15   Complaints

ALL shades of the community, including the middle classes,
the traditional supporters of the police, are now crying out for
all-civilian boards to deal with complaints against police. I
think that if this campaign is successful, I will smile to myself
and say 'I told you so.' The greatest safeguard that the public
have against abuse and villainy by the police is the fear, felt by
the majority of police officers, of hard nosed, honest police
complaints investigators. Serious complaints are fully
investigated. I have been on the receiving end of the
complaints system on occasions, from the complaint of
impoliteness, which is the standard defence by motorists in an
attempt to keep their transgressions out of court, to the more
serious complaints such as the George Davis affair.

Being on the receiving end of a complaint is an uncomfortable feeling to say the least. The officers dealing with the
complaint have all served on the street as working coppers,
they have heard it all before and bullshit is wasted upon them.
Nothing would have pleased me more through my service than
to have had my complaints dealt with by civilians, no matter
how well qualified they may be. In the police service the
complaints investigation officers are regarded as 'them' and
the recipient of the complaint as 'us.' There is no closing of
ranks on behalf of the recipient. Interviews are professional
and hard and soon reveal the cracks in the story. God help the
system when the police of all ranks, close ranks, against
civilian boards. If you go too far, the bent copper will be
laughing all the way to the tribunal. Corruption will go
unpunished, and the public will be the losers. Keep a police
presence on the investigating boards however much it goes
against the inexperienced grain. Police will, quite rightly, want
defence representation on such boards. If you couple the
experience of the officer, plus legal representation with the
inevitable closing of ranks against civilian boards, the complaints system, and the public will be very much the losers.

Oh, how I hated bent coppers! I thought Robert Mark was
the greatest thing since sliced bread when he took over the

Met and introduced the anti-corruption squad called A.10 Department.

I met him on one occasion. It was a pat on the head occasion for me. As I sat in his office with the bossman at his desk I felt no awe. He was relaxed and I was soon the same. He listened to me, postulating the factory floor point of view and quietly tore all my arguments to pieces, particularly my current opinion of the Police Federation, the policeman's trade union. I was impressed with him. I considered that during his term he had badly shaken up the small but vicious minority of bent bastards in the job. You'll never be rid of them altogether, but he did, at least, make them look over their shoulders and actively discouraged the more faint hearted of them from further skullduggery. I left his office as his confirmed supporter.

Some years later I met David McNee, his successor, in the commissioner's office under similar circumstances. What a difference! It was possibly me and my preconceived ideas about him that accentuated, to me, the difference between the two men. I did not dislike McNee as the bossman, I didn't have any feelings about him at all except for a considerable lack of admiration. His disadvantage, as far as I was concerned was the braying of the press as to the coming of the 'Hammer.' His impact on the copper on the street was hardly noticeable. The one thing in his favour was his non-appearance, after retirement, on commercial TV. In my uninformed opinion David McNee was a non-event at police station level. Mark on the other hand was either hated or admired depending which side of the fence you were on!

Wherever you have a police force you will have the opportunity for corruption. Because, for many many years, the Metropolitan Police had been presumed, by the public, to be incorruptible, it was possible for corruption by the few who hid behind the honest capes of the majority. The organisation did not exist to deal with these wicked bastards. Wicked bastards they were, because the main source of income for the bent cop has to be someone who is already deeply in the shit and who is willing to pay to be flushed quietly and safely away.

Before Mark there was nowhere for the straight bogey to go, should he uncover the machinations of the bent. As it transpired in the clean out, some senior officers fell by the wayside. These would be the men to whom the straight copper would have had to voice his suspicions. No wonder corruption flourished!

The vast majority of coppers with whom I served were straight, honest, incorruptible men. I have had, during my service, rumour and second-hand knowledge of alleged misdeeds by certain officers. Rumour is never any good, it requires detailed investigation to prove an allegation and, until Mark, the machinery did not exist. Most of the uniform men I knew wouldn't know how to be corrupt, and this naivety is often referred to scornfully by the bent minority. The public, as the result of sensationalistic media activity, did, at one stage, firmly believe that the Metropolitan Police consisted mainly of corrupt coppers, all milling about in their various cesspool activities, living in luxury and coining in their illgotten gains. The media were right, and always will be right, to have a go about bent police officers. If only their allegations did not always have to exaggerate the percentage of cops involved. One is one too many, you'll never really beat them, but you can keep their numbers down by constant vigilance.

In the climate that exists it is very easy for a villain, when all other avenues of escape are closed, to allege dishonesty by police in their dealings with him or her. So by all means listen to allegations against the police, but give the police officer involved the same criteria, as regards proof, that one requires when dealing with any other suspect. Allegations made against a policeman are very easily made, and, if not proved, leave a stain on his record that perhaps he did not deserve.

Chapter 16   In Black and White

ANY policeman who has worked for a number of years in an area where a large portion of the population is, as is popularly defined, an ethnic minority, and who does not admit, after a while, to certain prejudices, is not really telling the truth. If, as I did, a large proportion of each day is spent dealing with the criminal element of an ethnic community, then, human nature alone is sufficient excuse for the formulation of certain points of view.

I will put my cards on the table and admit that I don't like black villains, but then, I'm not overfond of white villains or even, if there were any, blue or green villains! Robbery, on the street, after dark, of defenceless old people, is predominately a crime committed by black youths. They rob black and white members of the defenceless community, they have no prejudice. Both personal knowledge and statistics prove what I have said. This may indicate to some that I am a racist, but had they been at my home with me on many, many occasions, they would have been able to see that a high percentage of visitors to my home, both for social reasons or in search of advice and help were of that same ethnic minority!

You must not brand everyone who has something to say about race a racist. If you do, you are doing the ethnic minority no favours at all. One becomes a racist when one's contact with the villainous part of a community influences one's attitude to those other, law-abiding members of the same community. It is difficult for the copper working a patch like mine to maintain his cool, when, time after time, he is calling for an ambulance, on his radio, for some poor old dear who has lost her savings in her handbag after an assault and theft. The secret, as far as policing is concerned, is to put it behind you after the job has been done.

It is part of the copper's mentality, with experience, to dislike the thief, the robber and the rapist, particularly as the copper's contacts with the victim are probably closer than any other government agency.

If the vast majority of the population on my patch were

coloured purple, then eventually I would have developed a dislike of purple villains. Those members of the black community with whom I came into contact, as a copper, could be equally divided between criminals and victims. If a drunken Scotsman caused me undue hassle and a bloodied nose, I would refer to him as a 'Scottish bastard!' He would call me a 'fucking sassenach.' After the court appearance and in more sober moments all this would be forgotten. Most people are aware that short Glaswegians, when in drink, are usually mean fighting machines, and can say so! Often to the delight of the little tough Glaswegien himself.

Unfortunately the same does not apply to our black brethren. Why? With Scotsmen there is not, lurking in the background, a self-appointed spokesman, who sees an accusation against a particular Scotsman as an insult to the whole Scottish nation. There are, however plenty to leap to the defence of the black, whatever he had done, purely on the grounds of his race, rather than the misdeed he is alleged to have committed.

I say, catagorically that I would not like to be a black youth living in London. There are pressures on the poor sod from all sides. He is not likely to be as employable as his white counterpart. His spokesmen are telling him to retain his national characteristics, to grow his hair in tarry ringlets and call himself Rastafarian. If that's what he wants, then good for him, but, the employer seeing this, to him, alien apparition approaching in search of a job, will be reluctant to employ him because the lad doesn't conform. There is no reason that he should attempt to conform, except to recognise that the British are a conservative, conforming society, and have been for years. Once this national characteristic has changed, life will be easier for the black youth and the white non-conformist with his parrot hairstyle. But, until it does change, he will have to meet us half-way and prove himself. Why should he have to prove himself? I agree, he shouldn't need to, but we are dealing with human nature and British human nature is a strange enigma. Legislation on racism is a mistake, it will widen the gap.

There was no legislation to assist communities who have immigrated in the past. The Paddy shrugged his shoulders and worked and drank hard and established himself in this country, without legislation. I have never seen the skies over Ireland and consider myself English, but I am of Paddy immigrant stock. The Jews, who have been villified since time immemorial, have established themselves without legislation.

Having looked, in some amazement, at the various campaigns that have been instigated on behalf of the ethnic minority, I can count on one hand the few that have been initiated out of a sense of grievance, rather than having been pushed by faceless people from behind, for a political purpose.

The only legislation that would enhance the racial situation alleged to be endemic in our communities, is, in some way, to regularise the self appointed spokesmen in the black community. Some are, of course, sincere, but lots, and I do know this from experience, have done very nicely, thank you, out of the misfortune of their coloured brothers. They have established themselves as upright citizens of good intent and as respected spokesmen. Has it occurred to anyone that should racial harmony be established, then these spokesmen would be considerably less powerful and quite a lot less financially sustained?

The left has, at last, realised that the easiest way to alienate the public from the police is through ethnic minority disputes. They are very successful; we, the police, have lost this battle, and are on the defensive. The fight, against odds, in Grosvesnor Square won the police a tremendous victory morally over the extreme left. They won't let that happen again. Police against National Front or Communists can sometimes assure a good press for the law, but police against blacks, however you do it, will ensure a bad press for the police and enable the far Left to leap to the defence of their black brothers. Both the blacks and the police and the public are being conned rotten by agitators and extremists who thrive on racial disharmony. They cause it behind the scenes, and then benefit from it afterwards. We are all being conned.

Chapter 17   A Villain's Wedding

I DON'T usually care much for weddings. But one in
particular will always remain in my memory. A local widow,
who was a very good family friend of ours, decided to remarry.
She was a lovely woman, down to earth, with little refinement,
but an absolute diamond, as Arthur Daley would describe her.
She was as straight as a die, but a number of her friends and
associates were, to say the least, a little way off the law abiding
track! I had no second thoughts about accepting the invitation
to attend her wedding, although I knew that some of the
guests, were they to be aware that I was Old Bill would be a
little, shall we say, tense.

Gigs and I looked forward to the wedding. At the time we
didn't have a car. The Saturday morning arrived, and, all
poshed up, we wended our way towards a nearby bus stop to
catch a bus to the registry office. As we arrived most of the
guests and both participants, had also arrived. The babble of
noise in the normally sedate foyer was more indicative of a
four ale bar than a place of marriage. Some of the language
was loud and juicy and other waiting parties looked quietly on
in some amazement. Then the chief guests in their uniform of
camel hair coats and trilby hats arrived in two large Jaguars. I
looked anxiously for the violin cases in which the sub-
machineguns were kept, but they were absent. It was, without
any doubt, the happiest, jolliest wedding that I have ever been
part of; the jokes the smuttiest, the grins the widest I have
seen. Throughout it all was a genuine affection, shared by
Gigs and I as well, towards the happy couple. Neither was
nervous. It was bloody marvellous.

As the bride and groom assembled in front of the registrar's
desk, the ceremony was about to begin, and the registrar leant
across to the bride, and, in a stage whisper, said, 'Take hold of
his hand.'

With a wide grin, and in a very loud cockney voice, the bride
said, 'Take 'old of 'is wot?'

There was uproar, the tone was set and the ceremony
continued.

After the ceremony we adjourned for photographs and then on to the reception. The address was carefully written on the invitation and we set out to look for it. The slightly shady lot in their Jaguars, and Gigs and I by bus. There is a moral there somewhere! We arrived outside the address given, which was on my patch. It was an old shop, with tattered advertising posters flapping on the hardboard covering the window. To all intents and purposes it was a derelict building.

'There must be some mistake here,' I mumbled to Gigs.

She looked at me in that way that only wives can, when they think the old man has cocked it up again.

Then, to our surprise, a little door opened in the hardboard covering and a beckoning finger led us through. To my astonishment we were in a fully fledged drinking club! I had worked then on the patch for 20 years, passed it every day on patrol, and didn't know it was there! So much for my knowledge of the area. The food and booze flowed and we had a tremendous time. Everybody seemed to know I was a copper but I had no harassment at all. The bride must have warned the others that we were her friends, and the etiquette survived the effects of gallons of booze. When, in later years, I retired from the police, I returned the compliment and she spent the evening amongst hundreds of coppers, accompanied by her new husband.

An occasion that furthered my knowledge of the social habits of the monied villain classes occurred without any prior knowledge. Gigs and I enjoyed it so much that I began to think that the only people with a half way decent sense of humour, were coppers and villains. I would certainly never have gone to this celebration had I known, but by the same token I wouldn't have missed it for the world. The journey started when the neighbour who had invited us drew up outside in his large Rover saloon and drove us off to an East End pub.

The party was well under way when we arrived. All the men were very large and confident, with beautifully tailored suits, though the cut was just a trifle flash. The women, most with bouffant hair, were absolutely dripping with gold. Whether the gold had been theirs from new, was a matter for conjecture. Again the babble of people loudly enjoying themselves. One round would have set me back a week's pay.

We settled back to enjoy ourselves; we were trapped in that we could only leave when our transport went. As the evening progressed I fondly thought that that the fact that I was a copper would go unnoticed. The knees up started, it was vintage East End. The bouffant styles began to slip slightly awry, and as I looked at the men there, I realised that though they would be magnificent friends, it'd be a bit dicey being an enemy. Being a copper I was in a slightly easier position because my gang was bigger than theirs.

As I drank up in my new found anonymity I noticed, in the corner, a broken nosed, vaguely familiar face, but not familiar to the point of name, or where last seen. Suddenly, the man unfolded himself to his full height, he was like a brick outhouse, and sauntered across to me.

'I'm not who you think I am, I'm his brother, all right?'

My illusions of non-recognition evaporated. I just looked at him; he winked and wandered off. Thank Christ I didn't know who he was, because I feel that any constabulary endeavour on that occasion would have meant, Goodbye Brady!

When the evening drew to a close, we thankfully left the pub. I wasn't too comfortable with them, wasn't inclined to be over friendly towards them, but, if I had had the choice, I would still rather be with them than with a similar number of barristers. At least these blokes were blatant villains!

Chapter 18   A Little Glory

THE morning mail arrived on a day in early March 1975. I was late turn 2pm to 10pm duty, and was lazing in bed sipping a cup of tea which had been brewed for me by Gigs. The letter-box clicked and the mail fell inside the front door. I was singularly uninterested and sincerely hoped it wasn't more bills.

Gigs came wandering into the bedroom a slightly puzzled expression on her face.

'There's a letter here from 10 Downing Street!' she said.

She handed me a long white envelope. I immediately thought, this is a piss take by the lads at the nick. I tentatively opened the letter which was marked personal and started to read,

In Confidence
Sir,
  I have the honour to inform you that The Queen has been graciously pleased to approve the Prime Minister's recom-mendation that the Queen's Gallantry Medal (QGM) be awarded to you.

There was some additional blurb regarding confidentiality until such time as the award had appeared in the *London Gazette.*

My first reaction after the initial pleasure at such good news was a slight feeling of embarrassment and hope that other blokes involved would be similarly recognised.

Other letters followed in quick succession, one from Roy Jenkins the then Home Secretary. I must admit that I felt it all a little overdone. Apparently this fuss was due to the incident involving my old friend Rudolph Hess who had done me a mischief with his shotgun.

Realisation dawned on Gigs and I, after a letter from the Lord Chancellor's Office, that we would actually be going to Buckingham Palace to do the business about the medal. This hadn't actually occurred to us in the initial euphoria. My pleasure was complete when I realised that my sons Michael and Alan would also be able to attend.

Finally the invitation arrived. We were to attend the investiture at the Palace 10am, Wednesday 16th July 1975. I knew that it was all true when Gigs nipped away and brought a couple of hats suitable for the occasion. At the time we owned a very old banger of a motor car which was about 90 per cent rust. The thought of driving it through the gates at the end of the Mall filled me with some trepidation. The coppers at the gate would probably issue me with about 20 summonses if they saw it. To my relief my governor at the nick informed me that we would all be transported there by the police in a job car. I have never been a very smart copper and was not surprised when they issued me with a decent uniform for the occasion. I even cleaned my shoes properly instead of on the back of my trousers. I was going out of my way to appear unconcerned and modest over all this fuss and palaver, but I was, secretly, very very thrilled for my family. Particularly Gigs, who had had to put up with so much through the years of my police work.

The great day arrived; Wednesday morning at nine o'clock, the shining black motor car appeared outside my place and we were at last on our way.

As always there were crowds on the pavements outside the palace. Gigs did her regal wave from the back seat, the coppers at the gate saluted and we were through. Gigs' eyes were shining, she was enjoying it! I thought of all the times she had been called out to hospital where I was languishing after some incident or other. I thought of her anxieties whilst I was at Notting Hill, or Grunwick. The trials and tribulations she had suffered when she had heard that I had been shot. The endless nights alone when I was, like other coppers doing night shift. The kindnesses she had shown to numerous old lags whom I had tried to befriend. The coppers and their wives she had befriended and advised quietly through the years, her unfailing good humour and quiet wit. I felt a little guilty that I was getting all the fuss. If anyone should be receiving a gong this morning, I thought, it should be her. To be a good copper's wife, a woman has to be a special breed. There aren't many of them which is why divorce is a very common end to police marriages.

As we walked into the building, the splendour of it quite overwhelmed me. I have always been an extrovert but I was quite subdued, not least by the Lifeguards lining the staircase. A man in a black uniform sent Gigs, Mike and Alan one way and I was joined by Ryan David who was also up for a gong. He led the way to a large room lined by huge oil paintings. Gradually we became a little less overawed by our surroundings and Ryan began to get into his stride. We were joined by an RAF Wing Commander and a higher official of one of the Australian states who were to receive accolades of some sort or other at the same ceremony.

Ryan had introduced me to the delights of Rugby Union some years before and I was, and am, quite enthusiastic about the game. He plays and I watch, a mark of the disparity in our ages. During our conversation with the Wing Commander and the Aussie, Ryan loudly informed them both that all other rugby players are poofs when compared with the Welsh National side, and become his usual slightly aggressive self when it was suggested otherwise. The Australian, a cultured man, asked me, pointing to Ryan, 'Does he go back into a cage when this is all over?'

A very tall man, again dressed in a black uniform came over to us and said, 'Follow me.' We have no trouble with the armed services on occasions such as this, but we feel that police officers always need a little rehearsal.'

In a quiet ante room, the magnificently uniformed man, in a quiet and friendly manner, ran us through the formality required at the actual presentation ceremony. I wondered where my family had been ensconsed. The crowd of impending recipients grew. I saw some members of the Royal Ulster Constabulary there. I felt like clapping at them, and I felt a little humble in their presence; they really knew what it was all about.

We were assembled in a queue, the posh folk and theatricals first for their awards. I really didn't envy them their

Knighthoods, in fact, I must admit that I felt more than
superior to them, not for what I was to receive, but I was very
proud of the company I was with: coppers, soldiers and
ordinary people who weren't jockeying for position in life. I
was with the type of people I would choose to be with and I
fought the desire to tell the Ulster coppers how much I
admired them. It would have been embarrassing all round so,
for once in my life, I kept my mouth shut.

At long last our turn came. As our names were called we
were supposed to march to the dais where the Queen was
standing, but typically we were of course, out of step. At last
we got there. It was a scene I want to remember. I had spotted
Gigs and the lads on the front row of spectators in the
magnificent room. That pleased me. The glitter in front of me
rounded off the day beautifully. The Queen looked marvellous, no other word for it. The two Ghurka officers on either
side of her were built like brick shithouses and I'm sure I saw a
superbly uniformed bloke holding her handbag. I felt sorry for
him. I was impressed with The Queen, she spoke with some
knowledge of the Rudolph Hess business. We had a chat, she
pinned the gong on my chest, or rather, hung it on a hook
previously supplied on our arrival. I felt all of the emotions I
thought would be foreign to me at that moment. I almost
burst. As we marched out a chap handed me the blue box in
which the medal would live. As we stood about outside the
hall, I looked down at the piece of metal, new and shining,
with its blue and red ribbon. I was pleased, but I tell you the
honest truth when I say that when I heard what others had
done to earn theirs, I felt that I had been a little over-rewarded
for what I had accomplished. That's no bull.

Chapter 19   Tall Story

THE most boring time for police officers is about three o'clock in the morning, mid-week. Very little happens and it is at times like this that the practical joking is at its maximum. Steve Hughes and I decided to enliven the nick on such a morning whilst in for our grub break. We gathered together the necessary paraphenalia to accomplish our plan. The gear consisted of a horror rubber face mask complete with plastic sores and warts, one of my old police capes and a large size police helmet. By putting the face mask on, then donning the cape I was able to climb on Steve's shoulders, and whilst sitting there, allow the cape to drape over his face. This produced an extremely ugly nine foot tall copper, the height was enhanced even more when the helmet was added.

We first ventured out into the station backyard to practice the balancing skill required and then took a walk. Now if a police officer meets a senior officer in the Met the customary salutation is, 'All correct Sir.'

This indicates that all is well and the officer has nothing to report. On this occasion two strange men, in plain clothes walked into the back of the station. In my nine feet state I saluted them smartly, shouted 'All correct Sir,' and promptly fell from Steve's shoulders in a heap at the feet of the two men. They looked at me in blank amazement, were not at all amused and introduced themselves as senior customs officers who were at the station on duty for a specific operation. I pointed them in the right direction, regained my position on Steve's shoulders and we wandered off into the night.

As we walked alongside the nick a figure loomed out of the darkness and I realized, to my horror, that it was our own chief superintendent making a night visit. This was often done without warning to allegedly keep us on our toes. He stopped and peered through the poor light at the apparition before him. Although I was in control of the top half, Steve was the governor of the feet end. I kicked my heels into him like a jockey urging a racehorse to greater endeavours, and mumbled through the face mask, 'Run Steve, it's the chief!'

Sensibly he turned on his heels and ran. Unfortunately although by lifting the cape he could see where he was going, he had forgotten to take account of our combined height. We hurtled down the yard with the governor in hot pursuit. I had just decided to disembark and have it away on my own toes instead of Steve's when he turned into the door leading to the communications room. The crossbeam at the top of the door caught me knacker high and with a scream I was deposited on to the floor of the comms room. Standing there looking still unamused were the two customs men again. I scrambled to my feet and followed Steve through the window out into the street. A fast 50 yard dash saw us both sitting in the canteen playing a game of cards.

Some moments later the canteen door opened and there stood the chief superintendent, slightly red around the gills. He looked straight at me and shook his head slightly. I stood up 'All correct Sir,' I said softly.

The door was slammed in my face as the governor stormed off.

As meal break time ended Steve and I were called up to the chief superintendent's office 'Stick to the story Steve,' I said. 'If he alleges that we were dressed up as a nine foot copper, don't say anything, just look at him as though he were a nutter, OK?'

Steve nodded agreement.

We strolled into the office and there was the chief, 'Ah Brady, Hughes, there is a customs operation on tonight and they want police presence, so you will accompany them.'

We turned and there, for the third time in an hour, were the two customs blokes. They didn't look too enthusiastic about the chief's choice of officers, but said nothing about our previous episodes.

We set off in our separate cars and met near a row of Victorian terraced houses, one of which housed the villains and drugs the customs were after. The senior of the two explained, in some detail, that they wanted to get in quietly without disturbing the occupants, as it was felt that the drugs would disappear down the toilet if they were aware of what was about to happen. His final words were, 'Silence is essential until we are inside!'

We crept up to the house. It was a four storey terrace, one of the floors being a basement with its own area in front. The front door up a flight of about 10 steps. The front door was Victorian, solid and strong and the customs officers started to attempt to pick the lock. I knew these types of houses and was aware that they could play about with the door all night, without a prayer of getting in quietly. The only two ways, to my mind, were with a sledgehammer, or by someone inside letting them in.

I stepped back and looked up. I saw that a first floor window was slightly ajar with a window box with assorted plants just inside the window frame. The customs men were whispering and fiddling about. I thought to myself that it would be a tremendous triumph if I could open the door from the inside for them. This would dispell the opinion they had already formed of me, as a fat, bumbling idiot.

I climbed on to the balustrade alongside the stairs and without a word to the customs men pulled myself up on the the wndow sill. I stood, somewhat precariously on the sill and bent down to take a firm grip on the bottom of the window to lift it and enlarge the opening through which I was going to climb. I looked down and saw the tops of their heads nodding away and felt a surge of pride because I just knew that I was about to prove the superiority of the police over the customs service.

Whatever possessed me at that moment I will never know. For some accountable reason as I looked at the partially open window I stepped back to admire my work!

I have since discovered that the distance from the window ledge to the basement area in front of the house, is 17 feet. Have you ever fallen 17 feet? It doesn't sound much, but, in free fall, human nature being what it is, it is impossible for the terror stricken mortal to do other than deliver a loud, terrified scream.

This I did, very, very, very loudly and for a long time.

The customs men leapt about like men possessed. Their precious operation was a write off, all because of this idiotic fat copper who kept falling about. I saw their white faces looking in my direction as I passed them. Horror and indignation written all over them. The only cheerful face was Steve Hughes, he was falling about in supreme enjoyment. As I approached the level of their eyes I did expect, at about that time, to stop rather suddenly. It came as a most unpleasant surprise when I continued past them and carried on falling. I had forgotten the basement area!

I was still screaming with terror, my bottle, to coin a phrase, had gone.

I stopped. There was a lot of noise. I wasn't dead! I looked up and saw three white faces peering over the balustrade at me. One customs bloke actually had his finger to his lips in a 'Shhhhh' sign. He must have been joking.

I then noticed that I was terribly wet . . . blood . . . I thought, my heart stood still. The smell was awful, I'm dying, I thought, my sphincter muscle was kaput, that's always a bad sign.

I stood up. I had fallen into a large, old-fashioned zinc bath that had been there since the year dot, and was full of filthy dirty rancid water. Alongside it lay the remains of an old car engine. My luck had held again, another of the nine lives; three feet either way and I would have been dead, impaled on an old Austin relic.

I then fell down again. The reason was that I hadn't quite got away with it. All of me, except my calf and ankle of my left foot had indeed landed in the bath, that portion of my leg was fairly badly damaged. There was a certain amount of activity and confusion at the front door of the house, I was past caring. In the distance I could hear the familiar two-tone horn of an ambulance, it was, of course, yet again, for me. As it arrived and the crew disembarked to load me on, they bent over me and almost in unison.

'It's the copper who was bashed by the pisspot, remember us mate, blimey don't you pong!'

As I, yet again, arrived at The Whittington hospital the mouthy ambulance man had informed all and sundry that the copper who some time ago was knocked out by a pisspot, was back, this time he had fallen out of a window and landed in a bath of filthy water. There was much hilarity from the staff at casualty, and from the various coppers who came to visit me.

The last visitor was Steve Hughes, 'You know Dave, it all worked out OK, in the end. When you screamed, the geezer the customs were after, came down and opened his door to see what all the noise was about, and the customs blokes got in after all. They won't be coming to vist you though, the boss customs bloke says he never wants to see you again!'

Chapter 20   A Birth Day

CONTRARY to popular belief, policemen are not trained midwives. They are, of course, well trained in First Aid. The ambulance crews in the Met area are superb at what they do, and there is a wonderful spirit of camaraderie between the two organisations, at street level. However there are occasions when the copper with no ambulance to help him has to exude a confidence in medical matters which is far from the insecurity he really feels.

Some years ago, with the arch practical joker Jimmy French as my crewmate, I stopped the police car outside a large terraced house, which like so many of the dwellings on the patch, was a little shabby and appeared to be divided into bed-sits. We didn't know what we were walking into on this occasion, as the emergency call had been from a distressed female, and the operator had not been able to decipher the cause of the trouble. The front door was open, so we walked in. The hallway was not too clean and the wallpaper was peeling. There were a number of doors leading from the hall and we stopped for a while wondering, not only who had called for police, but what it was they wanted. From behind a door we heard a woman's voice, 'In here officer.' She sounded breathless and a little frightened. We opened the door and walked in. There, lying on a bed, was a woman of about 30 years of age. She was dressed in a nightdress and was obviously very, very pregnant. 'Please help me,' she said breathlessly, 'I'm in labour and I think it's due any minute.'

'What's the name of your midwife?' Jimmy said, 'Can you remember her phone number?'

'I haven't got one, we've just come over from Northern Ireland and I haven't made any arrangements.'

Jim and I looked at one another with raised eyebrows.

'Right, Jimmy, can you get on the air and make some arrangements?' I paused, and remembered every cowboy film I had ever seen and said, 'Oh, and put plenty of water on, we want lots of hot water.'

What we wanted hot water for I just hadn't got a clue, but if it was good enough for John Wayne it was good enough for me!

We bustled about in apparent efficiency, at least it must have looked that way, because the lady started to calm a little between labour pains, which were manifesting themselves at intervals too close together for comfort.

Jimmy temporarily disappeared to radio for qualified assistance and to somehow boil lots of water, for God knows what! Then to my utter dismay, which I was trying to hide behind a confident smile, she started! She was already on her back and twisting about, I was leaping from the head end to the delivery end, or, as I described it later, from eyes to thighs. I saw the beginning of a head appear from what I presumed was the correct orifice and scrambled back to the head end. 'Bear down gal, you are doing fine.' She was making a fair amount of noise and probably didn't even hear me, but at least it gave me something to do.

On my return to the business end, I saw the baby begin to appear, and to my untutored eye all seemed to be going well. Jimmy appeared with two large saucepans of boiling water.

'What do we do with this?' he queried.

I looked at him and spread my arms with hands palm uppermost, head slightly to one side like a Jewish merchant, unhappy with the price offered. I looked at the lady and saw that the baby, which now lay between her legs, was still attached by the umbilical cord. I remembered being taught never to cut or interfere with the cord, but to check that the babe's nostrils and throat were clear of mucus. At that moment, thank God, the door flew open and in bustled a nurse. She wasn't all that attractive, but at that moment she was the most beautiful sight in the universe.

'Have you touched the baby?' Crisply and efficiently intoned.

'No Sister.' I promoted her, just in case.

'Thank God,' she said. 'Just look at the state of your hands!'

Behind her Jim was grinning and gesticulating at the steaming saucepans. So that was what the hot water for? Ah well, I had learned something that day. The baby was a girl, we left well satisfied.

We had done nothing at all, and had we done so would probably have done her a mischief, but all was well.

Chapter 21   The Burglar

ONE of the more despicable crimes is when an ordinary working class household is burgled by a member of the same working class. It's fairly rare to capture a villain whilst he is actually on the premises engaged in his criminal endeavour. This is mainly because of the particularly English attitude of 'I mind my own business!'

However, I remember well a particular incident of this kind when the householder would probably have been better off if the police had not intervened.

Householders don't often report suspicious noises, to the police. However, on this occasion, one of the species overcame his natural reticence and informed police that, though he knew his neighbour was at work, there appeared to be considerable activity inside his house.

Having received the emergency call over our radio, we quietly but quickly raced to what would seem at first sight to be the usual false alarm. I baled out and went to the rear of the house whilst my mate went to the front door of the informant next door. The side garden gate, leading to the rear of the suspect house, was a tall affair and bolted from the inside. It had sharp spikes protruding from the top, which, given my usual run of luck, indicated that some sort of disaster would ensue, causing irreparable damage to my wedding tackle, should I attempt to climb over the top.

There was a timber paling fence alongside the gate which appeared more secure, so I launched my 15 stone at the fence, intending to bound over it as I used to with similar obstructions during my commando days. Alas those days had long since gone. My belly creased itself along the top of the fence, with ample proportions of my fat body creaking and swaying on either side.

Slowly at first, but with accelerating momentum the fence began to tilt. As the fence crashed to the ground I slid forwards into the rear garden. I slid forward face down, and, as the bottom half of my body passed across the now horizontal fence, I did myself the most awful mischief in that part of my anatomy which I had been so anxious to protect.

I leapt to my feet, clutching my groin and whining like a dog in extreme pain. I could hardly take it out and have a look to see what damage had been done, because it would not have been in keeping with constabulary dignity.

The noise of the collapsing fence followed by my pitiful whimpers of abject misery and pain, should, one would have thought, alerted every burglar within 10 miles of my presence. However, as always an optimist, I limped around to the back of the house, carefully cupping my balls into the least painful position.

From the back of the house there protruded a delightful conservatory-cum-greenhouse. This area contained the only back door into the house. The other side of this greenhouse was a large bedroom window, double-glazed and unopenable! I looked into the rear window and saw a nicely furnished typical suburban bedroom. The bed was covered by an expensive duvet, the dressing table was a jungle of little bottles and jars of lotions and cosmetics.

Standing in front of the dressing table, slightly stooped and searching through the top drawer, was a man. The fact that he had started his search of the dressing table from the bottom drawer and worked his way up to the top, indicated some measure of professionalism. This method saved considerable time which would have been spent opening and shutting drawers. He was so busy it seemed a shame to disturb him, however, that was what I was there for, so I tapped on the window and as his head swivelled and his eyes encompassed a large tubby policeman gazing at him, I raised my right hand and wiggled my fingers at him in a friendly 'Hello' movement.

His reaction was perfectly understandable. He leapt some distance into the air. The pain, which had left my balls from the moment I saw him, must have, somehow, transferred itself to his rectum, because, as he came down to earth he immediately clasped his anal region and developed a most pained expression.

I told my mate, on the radio, to hang about around the front after having explained what had happened thus far. The burglar ran out of the room towards the front of the house, still trapped inside. He must have seen the other copper, because he soon returned to the rear bedroom.

We gazed at one another. He was reasonably well dressed and in his early thirties. But then, burglars are usually well dressed. They very rarely wear a striped sweater or carry a swag bag!

I smiled reassuringly at him, putting on my kindest expression, the one which said, 'I'm going to nick you, and, providing you don't piss about, I won't kick you in the head.' The expression has been described by those who were anti-police, as somewhat threatening. I indicated with a little wave, that he should come outside. I was still smiling. He declined with a vigorous shake of the head, 'Come out you bastard!' I shrieked through the glass.

Another shake of the head. I cannot lip read, but I had a rough idea that the words he was using were far from Christian in their connotation.

I decided to enter the building and arrest the bastard.

I looked at the conservatory, it didn't look too robust, so I decided to kick the glass door in and gain entry. I gave the villain one more chance but he again shook his head. He had obviously diagnosed my intention and stood, hands on hips, agog with interested curiosity.

Experience has long taught me that the shoulder is the worst part of the body to use when trying to force a door of any description. A bloody good kick with the sole of the boot near to the lock area of the door will usually do the trick. Putting all of my experience to use I charged the rear door, my rage at the non-co-operation of the burglar may have caused me to use more strength than was probably necessary. I booted with all my might, and as the door collapsed my momentum caused me to follow through and I was actually standing well inside the conservatory. I looked towards the back window through the now open door and shook my fist at the burglar. His nose was flat against the window which gave him a somewhat grotesque appearance. He backed off and disappeared into the house.

My triumph, at having gained entry to the back of the house, was complete. One more kick and he was mine! Suddenly there was a gentle rumbling noise, interposed with a high long squeak which could only be likened to the sounds of delight emanating from a mouse engaged in coital activity.

I felt uneasy, and so I should have, because in one second the entire conservatory collapsed around me. I lay on the ground bleeding from numerous cuts, part of the heap of debris and considerably pissed off! I leapt to my feet with a howl of rage and charged the one remaining obstacle between me and the burglar. As I kicked at the door, it swung open causing me to perform the splits in mid air, and this action rejuvenated and accentuated the previous groin injury. I let out a tremendous roar of pain and terror. The burglar, presuming the roar to be one of anger . . . immediately surrendered!

As he was being led away to the police car, my mate suggested that he call an ambulance for me and my cuts. I felt that perhaps I would, yet again, meet the same ambulance crew who dealt with the pisspot incident and the fall from the window job, so I declined. Instead I popped along to the nearby cottage hospital. I was suffering from superficial cuts to my face hands and legs, but was puzzled by a slight cut on my arse. This confused me because there was no corresponding slit in my trousers!

I arrived at the hospital to be met by the most sympathetic nursing sister, unlike the bastards at St Mary's who used to extract the urine.

She smiled helpfully,

'You will have to have an anti-tetanus injection before we do anything else,' she smiled and indicated a nearby room. 'Pop in there and get yourself ready.'

I walked in to the room stripped my shirt and jacket off and loosened my trouser belt. The sister, after a delay of some minutes, walked in with the tray and hypodermic needle. I dropped my trousers and presented the cheeks of my bum towards her.

'Very nice,' she smirked. 'But I want to inject your arm!'

I straightened up, red-faced; why did this always happen to me?

It was always distressing to attend a housebreaking. Most women are not upset so much at the losses they suffer from the hands of a thief, but more at the thought of a burglar wandering about in the home and defacing, among other things the privacy of the home. It is almost without fail, the primary emotion. I have known families sell up and move for this reason alone. It is an emotion that I can well understand. Men are slightly more philosophical about a break-in. Their main emotion is the desire to lay hands on the thieves. It is hard to find adequate reasons to justify (no matter how deprived the thief may have been in his childhood) an attack to the home of a family who have struggled to maintain it in some semblance of respectability.

We are often called to houses where a break-in has taken place, and the occupants are at work. I remember well such a call, where neighbours had seen the entry being made and called the police. On our arrival a quick search established that the villains had long gone. The place had been well turned over and left very untidy. Perched in an ashtray, on the lounge coffee table, were some packets of cigarette papers and a small cube of cannabis resin. They would hardly have been left there by the thieves, and the presumpton was that they belonged to the householder. Theoretically I should have made inquiries of the householder, and if it transpired that the substance was his, then I should have nicked him. I couldn't bring myself to do this. The owner of the house had been burglarised, his place was a mess. I had entered without his strict permission to search for the thieves. I decided that the only course of action I could take, rightly or wrongly, was to caution him about it. I therefore left him a note on the table stating that police had attended his property and he should contact us, on his return home, for further investigation of the burglary.

I left a further note, leaning against the cube of cannabis.

METROPOLITAN POLICE.
PLEASE KEEP OFF THE GRASS.

I then left the address and continued with my patrol. I hope, on his sad return to his burgled home the little note helped him to realise that not all coppers are bastards!

Chapter 22   Kids

THE greatest rewards of police work can come to you quietly and leave a warm glow that makes it all worthwhile. The old girl who, most Wednesdays, would pop into the nick with some freshly baked cakes as a present for the coppers as her way of saying 'Thank you.' (The sad part of the response to this kindness was that we did not dare eat the produce of her apparent gratitude, just in case she had put something unmentionable into the ingredients. Such is life!)

One of the most gratifying moments of my police career came without warning, and from the most unlikely source. It was worth all the medals in the world. A local lady whose husband had died some months previously was the proud parent of about five kids. She was as honest as the day is long and worked very hard to keep the family's head above water. The kids' lives were spent in an environment which would inevitably cause the majority of them, at some stage of their lives, to become guests in one of Her Majesty's Establishments of Correction.

I had had some dealings with the family and felt that, beneath the hard exterior the kids were really extremely likeable, providing you kept an eagle eye on your wallet whilst playing the heavy social worker with them.

I felt sorry for the kids, they had no chance. Mum stopped me on the street one day.

'Can I talk to you?'

'Of course you can,' I replied.

'I'm really pissed off with the way my kids are always getting nicked,' she looked harassed and sad, 'I don't want to talk to one of the young coppers, but could you have a talk to the little fuckers and try and knock some sense into them about always getting into trouble?'

I agreed to try and help. Through the years that followed, with the occasional chat, and more often a clip round the ear when they got lippy I managed to establish contact with the little sods. They were still getting nicked, but not quite so often. I remember the two snotty nosed lads of hers, on bicycles, cycling up to me whilst I was sitting in the police car.

'Hi Mister Brady.'

'Where did you get those bikes from? If you've nicked them I'll have your guts for garters,' I said.

Having established the legitimacy of their ownership I had a chat with them.

After a while they were about to cycle off, the eldest looked at me through narrowed eyes and said, 'We was talking about you. For a copper, you're all right.'

He went a little red and they both cycled away rapidly. That was worth all the medals in the world. I remember the lads, villains though they had become, with considerable affection and their mum as the salt of the British working class earth!

About 60 per cent of burglaries are performed by juveniles, and they have the native cunning of hardened lags. I remember one call on a summer's afternoon. The message told us that there were 'suspects on premises!' As we rounded the corner into the street and made for the address, there were, sitting on the garden wall of an adjoining property, two sweet little girls aged about 10, swinging their legs and wide eyed with innocence.

'Are you looking for two boys?' her blue eyes were wide with excitement. 'They came out of that house there and they've just ran round the corner.' She pointed up the hill.

I drove off rapidly up the hill and round the corner indicated. It led to a large block of council flats. I suddenly stopped. I don't know why. I reversed the police car and looked back down the hill. There they were the little bastards! Two sweet little girls, their elfin feature alight with craft, running down the hill away from me their arms laden with the goodies they had stolen from the house. I pulled up beyond them and stopped. I got out of the police car with my mate and approached them.

'We just found this stuff in a garden, we were taking it to the police station,' completely unabashed, having been caught in a hands up situation.

Subsequent inquiries revealed that they had indeed been

the suspects on premises we had been called to and that they were active house-breakers in our area. Their parents were, of course, horrified. As we were loading them into the police car we were conscious of the dirty looks of the local inhabitants and the murmurings that instead of harassing two little girls we should be catching burglars.

The other incident that stands out in my memory was as the result of a similar call by radio. We arrived at the address. Leaving one crew member watching the front we galloped around to the back of the semi-detached house. Sure enough, a window on the ground floor was open. I climbed into the window leaving my mate to cover the back. I found myself in a kitchen which had been ransacked and then heard movements from an adjoining room. I leaned out of the outside window and beckoned to my mate who came running. We quietly crossed the kitchen and, throwing open the door, we dashed into the room. With a courage terrible to see we faced our entrapped housebreaker, he was all of four feet tall.

'Who are you?' I asked.

'I don't grass to the filth,' his defiance encompassed every Humphrey Bogart film I have ever seen.

'Is that right?' I chuckled.

He drew himself to his full height, threw out his pigeon chest,

'I s'pose you are going to give me a thumping now.' The statement was made in a casual manner to indicate his worldly wise knowledge of the attitude of police to the criminal classes. It coupled amusement with sadness that this lad was, in his tender years, instead of playing cowboys and indians, screwing peoples' houses and being tough towards his arch enemies, 'The Filth.'

Chapter 23   An Unnecessary Dog

ANIMALS have always been a source of some confusion to me. I could never understand how something as large as a horse could allow itself to be domineered by a mere man. The sight of a large alsatian dog grovelling around its master doesn't fill me with ecstasy at all. Frankly I am quite afraid of large animals who have the propensity, at the slightest provocation, to change character and bite large lumps out of your arse! For this reason I always treated with the greatest of respect any call to which I responded that entailed dealing with any animal, large or small.

It was for this reason that I was far from happy to receive such a call on a Sunday morning. The call indicated that a large alsatian was in a very unpleasant frame of mind outside a nearby garage and was letting every passer-by know about it. The one saving grace in the whole situation was that my crew member was a relatively inexperienced copper, who could, with little guile from me, be induced to deal with the situation whilst I skulked inside the police car as a very uninterested observer, in complete safety!

As we sped through the quiet streets I was already formulating a little plan to enable my nefarious ideas to bear fruit. What I would do, I thought to myself, was, as we pulled up, throw open my car door and make as though to leap from the vehicle, hoping that my mate would do the same. As soon as he was completely out of the car I would regain my seat and firmly shut my door. I would then play the situation by ear. Good I thought! I then relaxed and accelerated towards the bloody dog's location.

We turned into the forecourt of the garage which was at the end of a cul-de-sac. There it was , Christ it was a large sod! It was leaping about and barking, with each bark I saw the long, yellow fangs and felt a little pang of guilt regarding my intended manoeuvre. Looking over nearby garden fences were various members of the public, agog with the possibility of seeing the local filth not only humiliated, but perhaps even, joy, bitten! I thrust open my door and started out of the police car. My mate did exactly the same in a reflex action and turned to face the dog. I slipped back into my seat and closed the car door. I do believe I may even have grinned whilst doing so!

The alsatian turned to face my mate. It growled and then, whilst it did not paw at the ground like a Spanish fighting bull, it certainly did, without warning, launch itself towards him. You could almost see the poor young copper melting. His whole body shook with fear as he half-turned to regain the safety of the car. I was making bets as to whether he would be able to make it to safety when a thought caressed my mind. 'Why can I see everything so clearly?'

With a start of absolute horror I realised two things simultaneously. I could see clearly because the bloody copper had destroyed my plan by leaving his door wide open when he disembarked. Secondly, my plan had placed me in considerable jeopardy, not him, because the blasted alsatian roared past my mate and jumped straight into the car, and on to the seat beside me. To compound the terror the devious bastard whom I had thought to be a pal, immediately slammed his door shut, so that the dog and I were encased in what I thought would soon be my tomb!

The bloody alsatian sat there, looking directly at me, its warm, foul breath pulsing against my face, tongue lolling and red eyes staring. I was transfixed with fear. Beyond the dog and out of the window I could see my mate's laughing face. He had been joined by a fairly large crowd of locals who had moved closer, full of anticipation. For them, now, the situation had unlimited possibilities beyond their wildest dreams. The radio suddenly broadcast a message, the unaccustomed noise caused the dog to snarl, and as I reached towards the radio the sudden movement caused the alsatian to snap at my arm. I felt that a heart attack was not too far away. The glee from outside the car was obvious, as more and more people joined the small band of spectators.

I pondered on my problem; if I could remove my carcase from the car and at the same time leave the dog inside, the problem would be resolved.

I tried various experiments. A tentative movement towards

the door handle caused a gentle snarling sound, with some teeth bared. It tolerated conversation without response,

'There's a good boy then,' was met with a complete absence of response. I noticed that the microphone for our radio was situated on the seat between myself and the volatile bundle of fur. Very, very slowly I eased my hand nearer to it until eventually, with extreme care I had the mike to my lips.

'MP from Yankee One, I have a little problem here.' I sounded like the commander of a space ship whose oxygen is running short. I continued, 'The wild alsatian you sent us to deal with is still wild, but is at this moment, sitting in the operator's seat like a time bomb. I cannot move, have you any suggestions please?' As the radio hummed the alsatian growled and barked which must have added weight to my snivelling plea over the radio waves.

I should really have known better. Every operator in every car in the Met had heard my sad tale. Lots of them were known personally to me and the response over the radio was disastrous. Barks and roars rent the airwaves, almost every-one can imitate the bark or growl of a dog in anger, and almost everyone did. The dog became extremely agitated and my bottle began to disintegrate.

The radio operator at Scotland Yard called for order and to my delight asked for any police dog handler listening to acknowledge. There was an immediate response from a dog van, and I became aware that within minutes I would have specialised help. My morale improved, and to demonstrate this improvement I smiled in a devil may care attitude at the small crowd around the car, hoping that they would interpret this as amazing cool under terrible stress.

I told the Yard that I was switching off my radio in view of the animal imitators who were auditioning over the police radio frequency and distressing the dog. We settled down together to wait. The windows gradually became steamed over in the warmth of the tension. I slowly wiped the window, to see a small blue van arrive at the garage. Out sauntered a dog handler, smiling sardonically at the inability of non-specialists in dealing with what was his particular forte. He opened the rear door of his van and out leapt a large alsatian, superbly trained and ready for anything.

As my companion, the alsatian, saw the police dog his attitude became rather strange; what I took for aggression was, as I was to discover, a different emotion altogether. His tail swished and his concentration on my behaviour diminished. The dog handler, meanwhile, had placed a leash on his dog and was strolling towards my car. He was, I must admit, swaggering just a little and almost nodding at the assembled crowd in a slightly condescending way. I sat there helpless and felt just a teeny bit humiliated by the whole affair. Still, honour was about to be restored to the tarnished image of the Metropolitan Police by the cool, confident dog handler and his magnificent alsatian. I then noticed that, clutched in the dog handler's right hand was a long, hollow pole with a loop of rope at the end. Obviously it was a dog catcher of some sort. Relief! My ordeal was almost over.

All attention was now focused on the approaching copper and his canine companion so I thought that about now was 'piss off' time for David. I threw open my door and flew out, closely followed by the hostile alsatian, barking like mad. In my panic, for there is no other word for what I was doing, I tripped and did a forward roll; this inadvertent acrobatic manoeuvre, I described later, as a deliberate and cunning change of direction to fool the dog.

I needn't have bothered. The dog shot past me and headed for the police alsatian. The dog handler's smirk flowed from his face to be replaced by mild alarm. I sat on the ground and watched transfixed as my dilemma galloped into some other copper's sphere of influence and responsibility. My various apertures gradually reassumed their normal shape and function. I felt relieved and well.

The crowd, which had scattered as I poured from my car, slowed, stopped and turned to see the next episode. I heard the slam of doors and saw that my young companion had re-established himself in our car with all doors firmly secure. Already I had forgotten that it was originally my intention to leave him in the lurch, but I felt a certain pride in his rapid assessment of the situation. He had the makings of a good copper.

What before had been controlled panic, now deteriorated to obscene disaster. The dog handler suddenly realised the intentions of my alsatian, and waving his dogcatcher endeavoured to save the virtue of the police dog. For, without any ado, my dog had mounted the rear of the police dog in what could only be described as a canine sex act without any preliminaries whatsoever. The police dog snarled and ran round and round, but to no avail. Now, my problem was that I didn't know the sex of the police dog, so was I witnessing the apex of sexual endeavour by a homosexual alsatian? The attitude of the dog handler had degenerated now to hysteria. He was shouting and leaping about. He was striking the homosexual alsatian across the buttocks with his dog catcher. We now established that not only was the alsatian a homosexual, but he was also a sadist, because the blows from the dog catcher seemed to spur it to greater activity than before.

I, in my new role as a witness as opposed to participator, joined in the boisterous applause of the spectators. Howls of joy emanated from the swelling crowd. Then suddenly, from the crowd, one voice, louder than the others, 'Rex, down boy, heel, heel!'

A man, recently arrived, detatched himself from the crowd, ran towards the alsatians, and grasping my old companion dog, pulled it clear. The dog handler, red-faced and angry, examined the rear portions of the police dog with much concern.

I wandered across to the handler, 'Thanks mate,' I said, 'I was in some bother there. Is your dog a dog or a bitch?'

I thought the question was reasonable at the time. The dog handler swung round, glared at me and said, 'Why don't you fuck off?'

I was quite hurt by his attitude and strolled back to my car. All was peaceful now. The dog owner apologised for the fact that his alsatian had escaped from his back garden, offered profuse apologies for the trouble caused. The beast of some

little while ago was now completely docile, wagging his tail
and licking his master's hand. Thus I never have since really
trusted domestic animals. That cute family pet of yours may
have, deeply enshrined in its character, both homosexual and
sadistic tendencies . . . you never know.

Chapter 24   Ambition

LACK of ambition is singularly unimportant when one is young, but, as the years progress a certain regret takes shape in my mind as to the opportunities I missed to better my lot in life. Men whom I have served with through the years and have passed me by to progress to higher things, have always been pleasant when they gazed back down the ladder at me, as they continued mounting rung after rung. I have never envied them, but, as I get older and the bills become harder to pay, I know that they were definitely right to choose promotion.

This fact was brought home to me recently when I was wandering in Norfolk and drove through the little village of Hethel near Norwich. It took my mind back over 25 years, back to Hornsey nick, when, as a fresh faced recruit, on a quiet Sunday afternoon, I was requested to go to the rear of 'The Railway,' a pub just down the road from the nick. There had been a complaint, from flats nearby, of excessive noise.

The interpretation of what is excessive noise is sometimes a little difficult. But generally the residents of Hornsey were not too prone to complain, except on Sunday afternoons. Sunday afternoons were sacrosanct as regards unwanted din. I strolled out of the nick, inexperienced, fully expecting to have to offer advice to a do-it-yourself enthusiast.

As I strode down the hill towards the pub it occurred to me that there were not too many domestic dwellings within earshot of the pub, which was situated on the fringe of an industrial estate. All was quiet as I arrived. I waited a while, then slowly turned to return to the station after what seemed another abortive call. Suddenly the air was rent with the most tremendous roar. It was obviously an internal combustion engine being revved to its limit. The noise was appalling and I felt some sympathy with the complainant. I quickened my pace and hurried towards the source of the noise which appeared to be a shed at the side of the pub.

As I arrived outside the large door of the shed the noise diminished as the acceleration was reduced. I knocked on the

door. It was badly timed, because as I did so the engine roared
into life again.

It was fairly obvious that the occupants would be unable to
hear me if I knocked till doomsday, so I opened the door and
wandered in. The shed was indeed a fairly large workshop and
was thick with fumes. Engineering paraphernalia littered
benches, with tubular steel and sheets of metal abounding. In
the corner, on a rack of some sort was the offending machine,
shaking and thundering away. As I peered through the gloom
a man, about my age, dressed in oily overalls was perusing a
large blueprint. He looked over the top of the sheet and
walked across to the engine. As he reached out to it a blessed
silence pervaded the shed. It was heaven.

'Can I help you, officer?'

I was extremely curious as to what he was doing, but first of
all I mentioned the fact that complaints were being received at
the station as to excessive noise. I also intimated that I had
some sympathy with the complainants, having been almost
deafened on my approach. Having established my reason for
being there the man was most pleasant to me. I glanced
around the shed. I am not one iota mechanically minded but it
seemed to me that the man was producing some sort of kit,
which, when assembled would be some kind of vehicle. We
had a general chat and I was offered a cup of coffee which I
declined.

I advised him as to the possibility of more complaints should
his noisy activities continue, and, just prior to leaving asked
him his name.

'Colin Chapman,' he replied, 'I'm the publican's son,' he
nodded towards the pub next door. With that, I left, hoping
that the admonishments regarding the noises bear fruit. As I
strolled back up the hill towards the nick I quickened my pace
as, behind me, I yet again heard the roar of the engine. I
retired defeated. It was as well I didn't linger, I would hate to
have been even partially responsible for delaying, even for a
moment, the aspirations of the man in the shed.

Back now to Norfolk some 25 or so years later. As I drove
through Hethel, behind miles of hedge I could see, in the

distance a large palatial house, and not too far away was the huge Lotus car factory, world renowned producers of luxury and racing cars. Who owned all this magnificent real estate and produced the superb machines called 'Lotus?' Why, none other than the same Colin Chapman of 'The Railway' public house, Hornsey, whose noise had so disturbed the local residents those many years before! I have never been so aware of my own lack of ambition.

Chapter 25   One More Body

SUNDAY morning. Early turn, finishing at 3pm, after a 7am start. Boring, boring. Nothing ever happens on a Sunday early turn. The drunks are sleeping off their Saturday night excesses. Dads are still in bed and haven't yet had time to indulge in wife bashing! The only people about are coppers and cats. The cats sniffing around the dustbins, and the coppers waiting to sniff into other people's business. After having been on duty for a very short period, there came a frantic call, by phone, to the station from a lady living in Stroud Green Road, alleging that there was a body leaning against the rear door of her address. She wasn't too happy about this.

I dashed off to my faithful police car and headed in the direction of Stroud Green Road. What a load of cobblers. Probably a drunk from last night sleeping it off. At the front door the first surprise was that it wasn't a lady at all, but a very effeminate guy. Society more informed and enlightened than I would have referred to him as 'gay.' To me he was a steaming poof. I haven't any hang-ups about poofs, what they do is up to them, I don't care. But I don't, if I have any choice, meander in their company.

His mincing expression could not disguise his terror. I started to enter the front door of the house, but Mincer pointed out: 'It's jammed against the back door from the outside, you'll only be able to reach it from the outside.'

I walked around the corner towards the rear of the house. Never run, I was taught many years earlier, unless you have to, it maintains a calm atmosphere. It works. I came to a dingy, blistered old gate which I passed through. Up a garden path festooned with empty beer cans and old newspapers. The grass brown from many years of pollution and lack of care. I was still slightly doubtful regarding the frightened demeanour of the effeminate bloke. All my doubts disappeared as I turned the corner of the outhouse which was attached to the rear of the house. At the bottom of a short flight of steps and hard against the basement rear door, there it was! No drunk this. It lay there, cuddled in the foetal position, on its left side. It was a collection of bloody wounds which covered every portion of his body visible outside his clothes. It seemed to me that he had either been kicked or beaten to death in the most brutal manner. I was conscious of a tremendous wave of sympathy. Not only for the dead man lying there, but also for the queer who had discovered him. I felt a little shame for my attitude towards him.

I could see streams of blood, now dry and coagulated, mapping their way under the back door against which it was lying. The stains indicated to me that he had been killed inside and then dragged out. He had been left there probably because he was too heavy to drag up the stairs. I can assure you that a dead body is a very heavy item to lump about. This one seemed to be that of a mature male. Beyond that, in the position it was in, it was difficult to deduce much else. I retraced my steps to the front of the house. By now a fair number of bogies were on the scene. With another copper I went into the front door and up the passage. It was a large house, full of bedsitters and with an absentee landlord. Fairly common in this part of town. The trouble with them is that most of the occupants of this type of premises are floaters and extremely difficult to trace once they have flown the coop.

It was obvious that the murder had taken place in the house. There were bloodstains along the passage where the body had been dragged; it seemed that that the murder had taken place in the front ground floor room. It was from under this door that the trail seemed to start. The outside of the door was smeared with blood and hand marks. I banged on the door, being careful not to disturb the hand marks . . . long wait . . . no reply of course. I carefully tried the door, it was locked. I had a problem; to attempt to force the door would disturb evidence, that I couldn't do. I left the house and peered through the window in an attempt to see into the room. I could see specks of blood and marks on the inside of the glass. There was a venetian blind at the window. I could not see inside.

A forced entry was absolutely out of the question unless the murderer was still inside. I thought not, I certainly wouldn't hang about waiting for the law if I'd been involved in any thing as horrible as this. Have no doubt about it, it was horrible. I was a very experienced bogey, but even to me it was unpleasant, if only the do-gooders and abolitionists could see this. Not like the telly, where the body is always clean and lying there as though asleep. No smell of excreta, no buzzing flies, no abbatoir on the telly.

I knew, it being Sunday morning that the CID would be some time coming. Once they arrived with all the murder squad paraphernalia, I would revert to the very small cog that I was. It was probably a good idea to chat around and nose out what I could whilst the shock was still vivid in people's minds. Up the stairs I went to have a word with the bloke (bloke?) who had discovered the body and called the police. He had departed to his room as soon as we had started nosing about. I entered his room without knocking. It was a miniscule bedsitter, though nicely scented.

'Do you know the geezer who is dead outside?'

'I've never seen him before, officer, honestly.' He muttered.

The suffix 'honestly,' or 'on my mother's life,' and similar such pronouncements please me. They are usually an indication that someone, whilst not actually lying, is probably bending the truth a little. The truth, requires no such embellishment under normal circumstances.

'Well, what the hell happened. Who lives in the room below, at the front of the house?' I asked, a teeny bit aggressively, but not too much, we don't want any tears at this stage, do we?

'It's a friend of mine,' he replied nervously.

'Were you in last night?' I asked, 'When did you last see your mate downstairs?' I continued.

'I don't want to talk about it, I'm upset.' His voice broke and tears filled his eyes.

'Look mate,' I said, 'I don't care how upset you are, there's been a murder done here. I want to know what happened. If you don't tell me what you know about it, then I'll get upset as well and you'll end up down the nick. . . . Is your mate downstairs a queer?'

'Well, he's gay if that's what you mean.' The tears dried.

'Tell me about last night.' I asked. I was slightly aggressive as I felt that this twittering object would react to verbal firmness.

With that, the words just rushed out. Would that they were all as easy.

'All right, I have seen that dead guy before. I came in late last night. I went to my friend's room and there were four of them in there, my mate was with the dead man. They had met at a gay pub in Camden Town and they seemed to like one another. Anyway, I started to speak to the chap that was killed. My friend got upset and told me to fuck off. So I did and that's all I know.'

I told him to wait in his room and went downstairs. He was obviously a suspect, but that wasn't for me to decide. The place was well covered by uniformed police, so he wasn't going anywhere. There in the passage were Charlie Hulls and Clive Box. The former a detective chief inspector and the latter a detective sergeant. I always got on very well with the CID, though I didn't like all of them. But I did like both the officers who had arrived.

'What's the score so far?' asked Charlie Hulls.

I told them what the current situation was, and about darling upstairs.

'I haven't been in the actual room where it happened, I didn't want to mess up forensic.' I concluded.

We all went to the passage outside the room and I prepared to continue my patrol as this was now a CID operation. From there we went to the front outside window.

Charlie said, 'So no one has actually been in that room yet?'

'That's right Guv,' I replied. I continued, 'I can smash this window if you like, climb in, then let you in through the passage door. I shall be careful, I won't fuck up your clues.'

'Go on then,' he said.

I didn't need a second telling. It was out stick and a couple of gentle taps and the glass quietly folded away. I climbed over the window sill and into the room after having pushed aside the bloodstained blinds. As my eyes became accustomed to the gloom I saw that the room resembled an abbatoir. There was blood and gore all over the place. On the carpet and all over the walls. Huge pools of blood lay underfoot. Various objects, bloodstained, that had apparently been used in the assault, including a blood stained electric iron, lay scattered about. I slowly and gingerly made my way through the gloom and towards the door.

Suddenly, out of the corner of my eye, I saw, or rather felt, a slight movement in the corner, where there was a bed. I felt a moment's qualm. Here I was in a room where, in the last eight hours, a particularly brutal murder had taken place. I clutched my truncheon a little firmer in a palm that had turned rather sweaty.

I screwed my eyes towards the corner. I measured the distance between myself and the door, outside which the other officers were waiting. Yes. There was definitely movement. A figure loomed out of the bed. My arse changed shape, half crown, sixpence it went. My immediate reaction was to hit whatever or whoever it was, and then ask questions afterwards. I stood there, indecisive and a little anxious. A voice, in a broad, rough Scots accent, sour of mouth and Glaswegian in its aggression, boomed out, 'Who the fuck's that?'

'Police,' I replied, hoping that the Glaswegian wasn't as they usually are, still in a fighting mood.

'Oooh Christ . . .' a moan, then movement as the mattress squeaked beneath his body. I measured again the distance to the door. It was obviously locked. He stood up. Ah well he wasn't that big, but then they are very rarely big, but almost invariably nasty.

He didn't seem to be at all distressed by the surrounding gore and impedimenta of murder. He waved one arm around, encompassing the whole scene and to my surprise said, 'It's down to me and my mates, I suppose they've fucked off?'

They had indeed.

I could now hear an anxious knocking on the door. It was Charlie and Clive.

'It's OK,' I called, 'I've got a body in here!'

I didn't realise that they didn't know what sort of body I had got, they presumed another dead'un.

'Well, open the fucking door then!' a muffled voice wheezed from outside the door.

'Stay where you are,' I called hopefully to my bemused alleged murderer.

I trod carefully across the gore, trying desperately not to disturb evidence. I dragged the door open and saw the somewhat anxious faces of Charlie and Clive in the passage.

'I've solved it for you Guv.'

Charlie snarled, 'Stop pissing about Dave and let me in.'

'Honestly Guv, this finger here,' pointing to Jock, 'has already put his hands up, or almost anyway.' This was their first indication that there was anyone else in the room, their faces were a picture. Of course I hadn't solved anything, I just couldn't resist it.

'Take him out Dave, put him in the car. Say nothing to him.'

Charlie looked quite pleased.

We walked outside. I was holding Jock by the arm. His hands were bloodstained. I made a mental note that no way was he going to have a piss, or wash before forensic examination. I was pleased because I thought the CID hadn't noticed. I was wrong. Charlie poked his head out of the door and said, 'Take him to the nick Dave. Don't let him piss or wash!'

Away we went to the nick. I was acutely conscious of the fact that I had achieved the prime ambition of most coppers, that of catching a murderer at the scene of a crime, with the body lying outside. A lovely feeling, professionally speaking. But of course I hadn't done anything bright. The bugger was waiting for the first one to come along. I was, as usual, the lucky copper and in the final year of my service. Well pleased. Then back on patrol.

Chapter 26   Retirement

AFTER retiring from the police, both Gigs and I decided, for a while, to get out of London and do what most folk do as they slow down with advancing years. During our search for our Utopia we happened, completely by chance, to look over East Anglia. We came upon a little country town and I noticed that old ladies wandered into the shops having left their bicycles leaning against the window. Their carrier bags were full of shopping and no one stole it. Their purses were in full view on the top of their bags, and they were still there at the conclusion of their shopping expenditions. Cars were left unlocked and the local police were treated with a respect that I hadn't seen for 20 years.

'This is the place for us,' we thought, and we were right. The pace is slow, though the people certainly are not.

One morning, travelling by car to my new place of employment, I was revelling in the empty roads, the sun was shining and the usual birds were twittering quite happily in the trees. It was idyllic!

I stopped the car outside a village shop to buy some tobacco. As I entered the shop the red faced, cheerful country shopkeeper greeted me warmly. We had some conversation about the weather. I thought to myself how much more pleasant this was, after the rush and bustle of London. No hard-faced assistant throwing the fags across the counter at me. I bade the shopkeeper a lingering farewell and he, smiling, hoped that I would call again. The satisfaction I felt, and the warm regard for my brother humans swelled almost visibly from me. All was well with the world.

I glanced down at the change in my hand before placing it in my pocket. I had been short changed by 50 pence.

Epilogue

IT was now August 1983. I had retired from the police and was living in the Norfolk village of Harleston. (I call it a village, but my neighbours would lynch me, if they thought I regarded it as anything less than a town.) I was driving back with Gigs near Bungay, when I saw something that caused me to brake a bit sharpish.

'What have you seen, Dave?' asked Gigs, with the implication that if it was a mugging or a bent motor, I wasn't to get involved.

'Just a minute, gal. I've got to have a quick shuftie at this garage.' But there was nothing criminal about the object of my attention, it was just one of those coincidences that stop you short in your tracks.

Across the road from where I stopped was a typical country garage with an old car on the forecourt, a black Wolseley 6/90. The garage owner was under the bonnet of another car, but he sensed my interest in the Wolseley.

'Good old car, that, boy. Been using it as a taxi. Not a bit of trouble out of her. Used to be a police car, up in London.' Not half it used to be a police car. When it was new, straight from the factory, it used to be Yankee One, one of the first area cars I ever drove at Hornsey.

I stood and wallowed in nostalgia, what a tale that old car could tell. The characters who had crewed in the front seats of the car, and the villains who had, from time to time, nestled slightly worried, in the comfortable back seats.

Coupled with the nostalgia that I was experiencing was a twinge of sadness and regret at the passing of time. Here was this old Wolseley, after a dramatic lifetime on the streets of London, now rusted and old, quietly fading into oblivion on the forecourt of a Norfolk garage. The similie with myself was inescapable. We had both been dashing about like blue arsed flies when we were in our prime, working hard and enjoying it. Now look at us. Both resigned to our lot, our inactivity in the quiet English countryside, the car going rusty, and me already grey and slow. It was sad. The sadness however was tinged with just a little pride . . . We hadn't done too badly had we? If that sounds egotistical, I don't give a monkey's. We were both a dying breed who would have difficulty surviving in the current jungle of law enforcement. Perhaps we didn't do as well as we had hoped, because my generation of copper has left the legacy which the current generation are trying to put right. Let's hope they do a better job than we did. But then, we used to have support of the public and politicians. No Hattersleys, then, hating police and aspiring to the Home Office. Still, the only consolation is that scattered throughout the Met are hardworking coppers, sitting in their high powered police cars, working their guts out, with no thanks, who, someday, may be able to retire gracefully and feel that at least they had done their best, inadequate though it was.